Tom Herzberg

BREAKING FREE:

MY JOURNEY OUT OF THE CULT

A Glimmer of Hope for
Those Affected and Their Loved Ones

Tom Herzberg

BREAKING FREE:

MY JOURNEY OUT OF THE CULT

A Glimmer of Hope for Those
Affected and Their Loved Ones

Bibliographic Information of the German National Library:

The German National Library lists this publication in the German National Bibliography. Detailed bibliographic data can be found on the internet at dnb.dnb.de.

Publisher:	BoD · Books on Demand GmbH, Überseering 33, 22297 Hamburg, bod@bod.de
Printing:	Libri Plureos GmbH, Friedensallee 273, 22763 Hamburg, Germany
Editing and Proofreading:	BookBright E
Cover design:	Nskvsky
ISBN:	978-3-7693-1737-4

Dedicated to my wife, my family, and my friends:

For their tireless patience,

their unconditional love,

and their faith,

that I would find my way back into the light

TABLE OF CONTENTS

Chapter One

INTRODUCTION

That could never happen to me! I'd notice right away if something was off! Sound familiar? It's comforting — but deceptive — to believe you're immune to manipulation. Yet the truth is that no one is completely protected. Cults and other manipulative groups can ensnare people from all walks of life and at any stage of life. Regardless of education, age, or personal resilience, everyone is potentially vulnerable. Estimates suggest that millions of people worldwide are involved in such groups. In Germany alone, experts cautiously speak of several thousand, although exact figures are hard to determine. The scale often remains hidden, concealed behind vague assumptions and inconspicuous structures.

Joining a cult rarely happens in a dramatic or obvious way. Instead, it's more like a quiet, creeping process that initially seems harmless and even hopeful. Maybe it starts with a casual gathering, a discussion group, or a workshop where you feel you've found like-minded people. You're seeking meaning, direction, a community that understands your passions or struggles. Cults exploit this deeply human need. At first, they appear welcoming, open, and genuinely supportive. Only gradually, as you become more entangled in their web of relationships, does the initial warmth morph into a system of subtle control, growing dependencies, and underlying fear.

Once caught in this current, you often fail to see how drastically your own thinking and emotions have changed. For family members, this gradual transformation is hard to grasp. My parents and friends sensed that something was wrong — they noticed my behavior changing: I withdrew, became more reserved, and distant. Yet without concrete evidence, they were left uncertain.

How could they have known that these seemingly harmless meetings were part of a strict, controlling community? How could they have discerned that the people who claimed they wanted to help me were actually narrowing my worldview? How were they supposed to help me without tangible proof?

This uncertainty — the lack of clear warning signs and obvious indicators — often makes it difficult for loved ones to step in early on. And as they search for explanations, they feel powerless, isolated, and frustrated.

In my case, it was precisely the unwavering love and patience of my family that ultimately guided me back into the light. My mother once told friends, while I was still deeply involved with the group, "My son is on a long journey, but I truly believe he'll come back." Those words struck me profoundly later, when I began to disentangle myself from the group's manipulation. I hadn't consciously heard her hopeful message at the time, but her certainty still resonated in the deepest corners of my heart. That unwavering belief in me was like a quiet beacon, able to pierce even the densest fog. It played a crucial role in helping me find the strength to free myself.

This book is for you — parents, siblings, friends, and partners — who are worried about a loved one who may be caught in a cult. I understand how helpless, confused, and even angry you might feel. You may wonder whether you overlooked something. Perhaps you also feel guilty for not having sounded the alarm or intervened sooner. Let me assure you: you are not to blame. Cults operate with cunning. They prey on people's desires, fears, and hopes, gradually and persistently pulling them in. Their manipulative strategies are often so subtle and methodical that it's virtually impossible for outsiders to connect the dots early on.

My goal with this book is to help you understand how manipulation and influence function in such groups. I want to make you aware of the dynamics that emerge between members and leaders, the psychological principles they employ, and why certain warning signs often become clear only in retrospect. My personal story is the thread running through these pages, but it's merely the starting point. I will walk you through the phases I experienced: from the seemingly harmless nature of the first meetings, to the tightening bonds, to the moments of deepest despair and fear — and finally, the slow, laborious journey back to a life of self-determination.

You'll see how important your role can be as a companion and support. Gaining insight into the inner workings and mechanisms of these groups helps you respond to your loved one with more empathy. You'll learn to ask gentle questions, listen patiently, and interpret subtle signals without feeling compelled to "prove" that something is wrong. This awareness and patience can become a bridge, one your loved one may one day cross to return to a world where freedom and self-determination are possible again.

This book is not an academic textbook but rather a personal account, supplemented with concrete insights and context. My perspective may be subjective, but I've lived it — I've experienced the reality that countless others face. I've ventured through dark valleys, and I've also learned that leaving is possible. It's this hope I want to share with you. When you understand the power these manipulative groups hold, you'll be better equipped to counter it — with understanding, empathy, and unshakable faith in your loved one's worth and capabilities.

Let's embark on this journey together. By recognizing the mechanics of manipulation, transforming blame into supportive understanding, and regaining our own strength, we create space for healing and new beginnings. Your love, trust, and patience are powerful allies — far stronger than any form of coercive influence. Often, it's the gentle but persistent hope of family members that provides the rope leading out of the labyrinth. And that very rope, the one you hold in your hands, can help guide your loved one back into the light.

INTRODUCTION

Chapter Two

THE BEGINNING

2.1 PERSONAL BACKGROUND AND INNER CRISES

When I finally met Maria, I was at a turning point in my life — a moment when inner turmoil and external upheaval collided.

At the time, I was around thirty and had tried multiple career paths, yet none had brought me a true sense of fulfillment. I was enrolled in a distance-learning program in business administration (in German, BWL-Fernstudium), but even that felt more like a temporary fix than a meaningful step forward. I had entered adulthood full of ideas, envisioning marriage, children, a close-knit circle of friends, and a well-defined life plan. But by this point, my dreams felt distant, and I was adrift, propelled by a constant restlessness.

This inner void was reflected in my family life. After a series of professional missteps, I had returned to my parents' business, seeking temporary financial stability and a space to reflect. Instead, I found unresolved questions about succession, a company caught between tradition and modernity, and a father clinging to old ways, while I longed for something new. Every discussion about the business's future escalated into conflict. There was no true escape — within our family dynamic, I was always involved. The weight of unspoken expectations pressed down on me. What was meant to be a temporary refuge became an emotional crucible.

Beyond that, I felt like an outsider in my own family. Once, my parents' home had been a safe haven; now, it felt suffocating, filled with unresolved tensions. While my parents and siblings remained a tightly bonded unit, I felt increasingly alienated. The togetherness I once took for granted had fractured into two sides: them — and me. That growing distance, both internal and external, was painful. I had always seen myself as a family-oriented person, yet something was breaking, as if my roots were losing their grip.

Professionally, I was in limbo. My studies no longer held meaning, and my parents' business offered no long-term prospects. I questioned what I was even striving for — why I kept pushing forward in a world of half measures and compromises. My friendships felt shallow; I had people to party with, to share small talk with, but no one I could truly open up to. I longed for someone with whom I could discuss life's bigger questions — my fears, my hopes.

In this apparent dead end, my interest in spiritual practices deepened. I sought ways to fill the emptiness — meditation, yoga, sweat-lodge ceremonies (Schwitzhütten), power walks. I experimented, hoping to find even fleeting moments of fulfillment. Sometimes, the idea of a universal energy brought comfort, but it remained elusive. The childlike Christian faith I once had had faded, replaced by a vague esotericism that offered hope but no real guidance. I was open to new influences, to people who promised security, meaning, or belonging. Looking back, I see how vulnerable that made me — how easily someone could have taken advantage of my search for answers. If a loved one finds themselves in such a crisis, it's worth being vigilant. That kind of emotional fragility creates an opening for manipulation, making it all too easy for the wrong person to step in and fill the void.

2.2 HOW CONTACT WITH MARIA BEGAN

During this unsettled period, I met Lisa. It was by chance, on a crowded night in a lively club — one of those evenings where you hope, if only for a few hours, to escape the weight of daily life. I was immediately drawn to her humor, her energy, the way she carried herself so effortlessly. We danced, we laughed, and whenever I was around her, I felt lighter.

Our chance encounters became plans, our plans became dates, and before long, we were in a relationship. Lisa had a deep interest in spiritual topics, and with her, I could finally talk about more than just the mundane. She spoke about inner growth, wholeness, and the search for something higher. It resonated with me, touching the same uncertainties that had been gnawing at me.

Before long, she began mentioning her close friend, Maria. According to Lisa, Maria was extraordinary — a mentor with profound insight into the human soul. She described her as wise and intuitive, someone who helped people unlock their true potential. At first, I assumed Maria was simply a confidante — after all, everyone has that one friend they turn to in difficult times. But the more Lisa spoke about her, the more intrigued I became.

Maria, it seemed, had answers to the questions that tormented me. Lisa's stories painted such a vivid picture that, even before we met, Maria already seemed to know me — my insecurities, my family tensions, my spiritual searching, my longing to belong.

When Lisa finally suggested I meet Maria in person, I felt a strange mix of excitement and apprehension. What I didn't realize then was that Maria already knew all about my vulnerabilities. Today, I can see how carefully orchestrated it all was — before I ever stepped into her world, the power imbalance was already in place. She knew exactly where my weaknesses lay and could hone in on them from the very first conversation.

For anyone concerned about a loved one, take note: if someone who claims to help already possesses an uncanny understanding of your relative's struggles, it may be a warning sign of strategic manipulation. Information that seems harmless at first can later be used to gain trust and forge deep emotional ties — bonds that are far harder to break than they appear.

2.3 FIRST ENCOUNTER AND INITIAL FASCINATION

I remember our first meeting vividly. Lisa and I drove out to the countryside on a late summer day, heading to the place where Maria lived. Her house stood on a hill, surrounded by woods and fields. The atmosphere was peaceful — almost otherworldly. Even as we stepped inside, I felt an unsettling mix of comfort and unfamiliarity.

Maria opened the door with a smile, greeting me as if she had known me forever. Her voice was warm, her presence magnetic, and the way she listened — so intensely attentive — made me feel instantly understood.

She asked the very questions I had yet to answer for myself, touching on my deepest fears and hopes. She spoke of spiritual wholeness, ethical values, and a sense of responsibility toward people, animals, and the environment. She wove spiritual ideas together with health and ecological concerns, painting a vision of a more harmonious world. Nothing about her words felt forceful or dogmatic. Instead, she gave the impression of merely guiding me toward self-discovery. Looking back, I realize it was precisely this subtlety that made her manipulation so effective. I believed I was acting independently, making my own choices, while she was already steering me in a specific direction.

Her aura was mesmerizing. She paired a sympathetic smile with what seemed like genuine empathy. A casual touch on my arm, a direct gaze, a shared laugh at a lighthearted anecdote — each gesture fostered an immediate sense of closeness. I felt drawn into her presence, as if she were creating a protective space where, at last, someone truly saw me and took my worries seriously.

I was especially struck by how effortlessly she engaged with my spiritual interests. She spoke of her own experiences, of her belief that a plant-based diet nurtured both the planet and the soul. She referenced Christian values without rigid doctrine, encouraging me to connect my belief in universal energy with deeper spiritual insights.

To me, these conversations felt like an awakening. Finally, someone who untangled my chaotic thoughts, who understood my insecurities, who seemed to offer me a way out of the maze. Yet, in hindsight, it was this very effortlessness that should have set off alarm bells. The way she so precisely addressed my longings was no coincidence — it was part of a carefully crafted strategy. She had information. She knew what moved me. Her charisma, combined with her well-prepared insights, was a trap I willingly stepped into.

For loved ones, recognizing this pattern is crucial: when a new acquaintance gains deep trust in an unusually short time, appears to see straight into your relative's innermost thoughts, and simultaneously offers safety, meaning, and belonging, it can be a red flag. Especially during a crisis — when someone is searching for stability and direction — such a person presents a dangerously tempting offer. They fill an emptiness the vulnerable individual may not even realize exists.

In my case, emotional crises, family tensions, and a spiritual quest had merged to create the perfect breeding ground for Maria's influence. I was grateful to have found someone who seemed to accept me without judgment and truly understand me. What I didn't see then was that these initial positive impressions were only the first step — leading me into years of dependence, manipulation, and emotional exploitation.

Chapter in Brief

LOOKING BACK, THIS PHASE OF MY LIFE CREATED THE PERFECT WIN-
DOW OF OPPORTUNITY FOR MARIA TO EXERT HER INFLUENCE. MY IN-
NER STATE — MARKED BY CAREER UNCERTAINTY, FAMILY PRESSURE,
AND SPIRITUAL AIMLESSNESS — LEFT ME ESPECIALLY RECEPTIVE TO
HER MESSAGES. WITHOUT MEANING ANY HARM, LISA ACTED AS A
FACILITATOR, PROVIDING MARIA WITH VALUABLE INSIGHTS THAT SHE
WOULD LATER USE STRATEGICALLY TO DRAW ME INTO HER SPHERE.
OUR FIRST ENCOUNTER FELT HARMLESS, EVEN LIBERATING. BUT THE
EARLY WARNING SIGNS WERE ALREADY THERE — THE UNUSUALLY
FAST SENSE OF CLOSENESS, THE PROFOUND EMPATHY THAT LACKED
ANY CLEAR FOUNDATION, AND THE SUBTLE EXPLOITATION OF MY
VULNERABILITIES.

WHAT FAMILY MEMBERS CAN DO

For loved ones, my experience offers an important lesson in recognizing manipulative influences early on. If someone close to you suddenly starts raving about a new acquaintance who gains their trust at an unusually rapid pace, delivers seemingly perfect answers, and effortlessly soothes deep emotional wounds, it's time to be cautious. What appears to be genuine support could, in reality, be part of a calculated effort — where personal information is gathered and used to exert increasing control.

My own introduction to Maria illustrates just how easily a person in a vulnerable phase can be drawn in by a charismatic figure. At the time, it all felt like fate: I had finally found understanding, companionship, and meaning. What I didn't realize was how fragile my sense of self-determination had already become.

THE BEGINNING

Chapter Three

DEVELOPMENT OF THE SECT

3.1 PERSONAL ONE-ON-ONE SESSION – THE CORNERSTONE OF DEPENDENCY

When I first stood in front of Maria's house, the afternoon was warm and sunlit. A lovingly tended garden surrounded the small bungalow on the outskirts of town — birds chirped, a gentle breeze stirred the leaves, and the air carried the scent of late summer. Before I could knock, Maria had already opened the door, greeting me with a warm, welcoming smile. Her bright eyes and calming voice made me feel instantly at ease — almost as if she had been expecting me. In a way, I suppose she had.

Inside, her practice room was also her living room: airy and bright, furnished with soft, upholstered seating, illuminated by candlelight, and infused with the subtle scent of lavender and sandalwood. Spiritual symbols adorned the walls, crystals shimmered on the shelves, and small statues and mystical images created an atmosphere that felt both comforting and sacred. She invited me to settle in, gesturing toward the couch. "Feel completely at home," she said, and there was something in her voice that touched me deeply.

The first session began with breathing exercises. Maria's soothing words guided me into my own body, helping me release tension — each exhale feeling like a quiet shedding of emotional burdens. She led me through a guided meditation, asking me to close my eyes and travel to places of inner security. Under her direction, old memories resurfaced — some painful, some beautiful. Tears ran down my cheeks, yet Maria did not judge; she offered no commentary. She simply held space, encouraging me to let even the most difficult emotions rise and flow. Her compassion felt so real, as though she saw something in me I could barely perceive myself.

She never mentioned any formal qualifications, offered no written contract, and left payment arrangements vague, yet none of that seemed to matter at the time. There was an unspoken agreement: I trusted her because she was so convincing. The feeling of finally being understood outweighed any lingering skepticism. She handed me a journal, suggesting I record my thoughts so we could explore them further in future sessions. She spoke of healing on all levels — physical, mental, and spiritual — of aligning with higher energies, of living in harmony with the universe. Her quiet confidence, her serenity, and the warmth she exuded wrapped around me like a balm after a long period of inner searching.

These one-on-one sessions laid the foundation for a bond of trust that deepened with each visit. Yet at the same time, there were no clear parameters — no formal agreements, no evidence of credentials, no transparent fees. Instead, a dynamic emerged in which I became increasingly dependent on her, while she seamlessly played the role of a wise and selfless guide.

Today, I understand how pivotal that phase was. Back then, it felt like an anchor — something solid in a life filled with uncertainty. But in reality, it was the beginning of my dependence, carefully laid brick by brick.

Subchapter in Brief

THE FIRST PERSONAL SESSIONS CREATED TRUST AND EMOTIONAL
CLOSENESS, ALL WITHOUT ANY FORMAL GUIDELINES. THIS IS OFTEN
WHERE A FATEFUL DEPENDENCY CAN TAKE ROOT. FAMILY MEM-
BERS SHOULD BE WARY WHEN ADVISORS DO NOT DISCLOSE CLEAR
PROFESSIONAL QUALIFICATIONS AND QUICKLY DEMAND PERSONAL
TRUST.

3.2 THE STEP-BY-STEP SHIFT FROM COUNSELING TO A SECT – SUPERNATURAL REVELATIONS

After a few meetings, Maria began revealing more and more of her world to me. It was as if she were slowly drawing back a curtain, exposing secrets that supposedly only the chosen could understand. At first, they came as casual hints — mentions of her ability to speak with angels, of perceiving things hidden to others. Later, she spoke of visions and prophecies, claiming to foresee future events. Eventually, she confided in me about encounters with demons — even Lucifer himself — whom she claimed was pursuing her.

Her stories were both mesmerizing and unsettling. Whenever she spoke of the sacred messages she received, her voice would drop to a near whisper, taking on a conspiratorial tone. She told me about her childhood, when she had first sensed her unusual abilities, and about the traumatic experiences that had deepened her gift while also making her life more difficult. I felt a surge of both sympathy and admiration: How brave she was to speak so openly of her suffering! How extraordinary her spiritual power must be to withstand it all!

My willingness to believe was reinforced by my then-girlfriend, who was just as captivated and who affirmed Maria's extraordinary gifts. This dynamic only strengthened my conviction that Maria truly had access to hidden truths. Any rational doubts I might have had were drowned out by my longing for deeper answers. The authority she projected, the weight of her claims, the quiet rituals, the promise of spiritual healing — it all blended together in my mind, forming a vision in which Maria held a special, almost supernatural role.

Subchapter in Brief

THROUGH GRADUAL REVELATIONS ABOUT SUPERNATURAL ABILITIES, MARIA CREATED A MYSTICAL IMAGE OF HERSELF. FAMILY MEMBERS SHOULD TAKE NOTICE IF LOVED ONES SUDDENLY BELIEVE IN EVER-MORE FANTASTICAL SPIRITUAL PHENOMENA LINKED TO A CHARISMATIC LEADER..

3.3 THE STEALTHY FORMATION OF A SECT – FROM IDEOLOGY TO CONTROL

Over time, Maria's tales grew more grandiose. She claimed to be the re-incarnation of Mary Magdalene, a close confidante of Jesus himself. She insisted that God and the Archangels spoke directly to her, while dark forces conspired to stand in her way. These assertions placed her at the pinnacle of a cosmic hierarchy, where light and darkness waged battle for human souls — and she alone stood as the ultimate authority.

But this ideology was more than just a captivating narrative. From it, Maria began crafting strict rules and dogmatic teachings. Purity laws and special prayers were introduced — rituals designed primarily to exalt her. Any criticism was dismissed as proof of dark influences; doubt was labeled betrayal. My initial openness gradually shifted into quiet submission. Afraid of losing her approval, I clung to my role as a devoted follower of this "sacred mission," asking fewer and fewer questions.

The sect did not form through a single revelation but through a slow, insidious process. Step by step, my critical thinking faded, replaced by an unquestioning acceptance of her words as absolute truth. In the end, I found myself ensnared in a carefully woven web of beliefs — one that Maria had spun around us with great subtlety.

Subchapter in Brief

THROUGH INCREASINGLY DOGMATIC TEACHINGS, MARIA ESTABLISHED
HERSELF AS THE HIGHEST AUTHORITY. FAMILY MEMBERS SHOULD BE
SUSPICIOUS IF SOMEONE PRESENTS THEMSELVES AS GOD'S CHOSEN
ONE, DEMONIZES CRITICISM, AND DISMISSES ANY QUESTIONING AS
MALEVOLENT, OUTSIDE INFLUENCE.

3.4 FROM A SMALL CIRCLE TO A STRICTLY RUN SECT – STRUCTURE, DAILY LIFE, AND CONTROL

What had initially seemed like a loose spiritual community gradually hardened into a strictly organized sect with rigid hierarchies. Maria deliberately assigned roles: Some of us became her closest confidants, organizers, and assistants, while others were relegated to everyday tasks — cooking, cleaning, running errands. For a long time, I served as her driver, always on call. Every activity, no matter how mundane, was framed as part of a higher plan. Yet the relentless pressure, the demand for constant availability, and the endless, often meaningless research tasks drained my time and energy. Any success was credited solely to Maria, while every failure was placed squarely on us. The constant weight of guilt wore us down, bit by bit.

Group rituals and prayers bound us even more tightly together. We were required to "love Maria" daily, proving our devotion through hours-long prayers. She claimed to sense our negative thoughts and doubts. Disobedience was met with public criticism or sanctions. In extreme cases — as absurd as it sounds — even physical punishment was threatened or carried out. Threats, humiliation, and the constant surveillance of our phones and messaging apps created an atmosphere of fear. We policed one another, reporting any perceived transgressions. Friendships and family ties were severed — our "original families" were cast as enemies, corrupted by Lucifer, while Maria was elevated as our sole protector.

In this state of isolation and dependency, we gradually lost our sense of normalcy.

Loved ones often recognize these patterns too late: constant availability, complete submission to a "guru," withdrawal from the outside world, and growing distrust of outsiders. When you see these warning signs, vigilance is essential.

Subchapter in Brief

THE GROUP TURNED INTO A SECT WITH STRICT RULES, 24/7 SURVEIL-
LANCE, ISOLATING RITUALS, AND TOTAL CONTROL BY MARIA. FOR
OUTSIDERS, RED FLAGS INCLUDE TOTAL LOSS OF SELF-DETERMINA-
TION, CUTTING CONTACT WITH FAMILY, AND THE CLAIM THAT SAFETY
CAN ONLY BE FOUND WITHIN THE GROUP.

3.5 PERSONAL CHANGES, INITIAL DOUBTS –
AND THE DIFFICULTY OF LEAVING

Under this regime, I lost my sense of self. My humor, my spontaneity, my former hobbies — all of it faded as my life became dictated entirely by Maria's demands. I lived in constant fear of dark forces, saw hidden signs everywhere, and interpreted every unusual event as a spiritual omen. Depression, insomnia, and physical ailments became my daily companions. The belief that I could not survive in the hostile outside world without Maria's protection took deep root in my mind.

Tiny doubts did begin to surface, but they were swallowed by paralyzing fear. Leaving the group felt impossible. Maria had made us economically dependent, burdened us with guilt, and warned that we would perish if we ever left. Even when I questioned whether it could all be true, fear suffocated me. Who walks away from a sect without plunging into the unknown? Besides, the mere thought of escape was framed as Lucifer's influence — a sinister force trying to drag our souls into ruin.

For family members, recognizing these behavioral shifts is critical. If a loved one is consumed by fear, severs all past relationships, surrenders financial control, rejects any criticism, and fully submits to a charismatic leader, it is a clear warning sign. Leaving such a situation often requires careful, external support, as those affected no longer trust their own judgment. What they need most is understanding, patient offers of help, and neutral, safe spaces where they can begin to rediscover themselves.

Subchapter in Brief

THE SECT DESTROYED MY PERSONALITY, ISOLATED ME FROM FAMI-
LY AND FRIENDS, AND CREATED BOTH FINANCIAL AND EMOTIONAL
DEPENDENCIES. DOUBTS WERE SEEN AS BETRAYAL, AND LEAVING
SEEMED UNTHINKABLE. FAMILY MEMBERS OFTEN RECOGNIZE THESE
BEHAVIORS THROUGH EXTREME FEAR, FINANCIAL EXPLOITATION, AND
TOTAL WITHDRAWAL.

Chapter Summary

THIS CHAPTER ILLUSTRATES HOW SEEMINGLY HARMLESS AND AP-
PARENTLY BENEFICIAL ONE-ON-ONE SESSIONS CAN EVOLVE INTO A
CULT-LIKE DYNAMIC. AT FIRST, THERE IS JUST ONE PERSON APPEAR-
ING AS A WISE COUNSELOR — WITHOUT FORMAL CREDENTIALS BUT
WITH GREAT EMPATHY. GRADUALLY, REVELATIONS ABOUT SUPERNAT-
URAL POWERS INCREASE TRUST IN THIS LEADER. STRICTER RULES
SOON FOLLOW, ALONG WITH TIGHTER CONTROL, FORCED RITU-
ALS, AND ULTIMATELY COMPLETE SUBMISSION TO HER AUTHORITY.
MEMBERS GRADUALLY LOSE THEIR FREEDOM, IDENTITY, AND SOCIAL
CONNECTIONS — UNTIL THE THOUGHT OF LEAVING BECOMES INCON-
CEIVABLE.

WHAT FAMILY MEMBERS CAN DO

Family members can help by recognizing warning signs early: a charismatic individual who portrays themselves as chosen, proclaims revelations, condemns criticism, isolates people from their environment, creates financial dependencies, and applies psychological pressure to group members. Recognizing these patterns in time can prevent a simple counseling session from turning into a deeply manipulative, exploitative structure. Supporting affected individuals requires caution and patience, offering them new perspectives and outside help — so they can find their way back to freedom and their own identity.

Chapter Four

LIFE
IN
THE CULT

4.1 DAILY LIFE AND ROUTINES IN THE CULT

Strict Morning Rituals and Spiritual Duties

Every day in the cult began under Maria's strict direction. From the moment I woke up, I felt pressured to adhere to her rigid routines. There was no gentle easing into the day — no personal choice of music, no space for free-flowing thoughts.

Instead, I would sit on the floor of my small room, fold my hands, and repeat the mantras she had prescribed. One central prayer was: "Maria, I love you." This seemingly simple phrase became a daily ritual — some mornings I repeated it for twenty minutes, other times for over an hour. The goal was clear: to align my mind with hers, to suppress any lingering doubts, and to silence my own desires.

Each morning, I was also required to ask for "truth." But this was not an open pursuit of understanding — it was truth as defined by Maria, shaped entirely by her teachings.

These routines and exercises served a singular purpose: to make me compliant, to reinforce my belief that Maria — whom I had come to see as divinely appointed, perhaps even a modern-day Mary Magdalene — was my only path to spiritual purity. I treated her as if she truly were the holy figure she claimed to be, convinced she carried out God's will and was guiding me toward a higher understanding. Any doubts that surfaced were swiftly buried. I had internalized the story of Jesus, Mary Magdalene, and our supposed divine mission so completely that questioning Maria's authority felt like betraying my faith.

Group Meetings and Constant Availability

Several times a week, we gathered for group telephone prayers. Often, we would wait for hours just to exchange a few words with Maria. These delays heightened our nervous anticipation, reinforcing our dependence on her. Actual one-on-one conversations were rare — everything revolved around her spiritual messages. "Reflection rounds," which frequently stretched on for three or four hours, were designed to assess our progress and ensure we remained in full alignment with her directives.

At the same time, I was expected to be reachable at all times. Whether I was at work or in the few private moments I had, any message from Maria took priority. It was common for her to contact me during my job, either to reprimand a member for an alleged mistake or to share a new "insight" about Lucifer (Luzifer in German) or her divine mission. Any delay in my response was noted. Waiting was not acceptable to her. If I did not react quickly enough, she accused me of neglecting her, hindering her divine work, or harboring selfish thoughts.

This created a constant state of pressure. Though my job had no connection to the sect, Maria's influence dictated my schedule.

Never-Ending Tasks

Beyond spiritual obligations, Maria ensured we were constantly occupied with tasks — grocery shopping, cooking, cleaning her apartment, driving her wherever she needed to go. Each of these responsibilities served as a tool for control. Even trivial errands — like the months-long search for a specific type of mattress — stretched into endless loops. There was never a moment to pause, never time to reflect critically

Spontaneous Sessions and Emotional Pressure

In addition to scheduled rituals, Maria frequently initiated impromptu meetings. Without warning, I was expected to drop everything. She would claim she was under attack from Lucifer or call out a member's supposed mistakes. These sessions could last for hours, culminating in an oppressive atmosphere of guilt and shame. We lived in a state of constant alertness, leaving no room for our own plans or free time.

Limited Leisure and Total Control Over Personal Time

Real leisure time was almost nonexistent. If there was a brief window of free time, I was expected to use it for "further spiritual development." Any activity that seemed unproductive was met with criticism.

I felt so trapped that I no longer recognized what real freedom looked like. Even in solitude, my mind was consumed by Maria's expectations. The fear of her accusations — should I fail to respond immediately or overlook something seemingly insignificant — kept me in a relentless state of tension.

Subchapter in Brief

THE DAILY ROUTINE CONSISTED OF A STRICT CYCLE OF PRAYERS, DUTIES, AND SPONTANEOUS MEETINGS. THERE WAS NO ROOM FOR INDEPENDENT THOUGHT OR PERSONAL INTERESTS. FOR FAMILY MEMBERS OR FRIENDS ON THE OUTSIDE, IT'S IMPORTANT TO NOTE: WHEN SOMEONE VIRTUALLY HAS NO FREE TIME, IS CONSTANTLY ASSIGNED NEW TASKS, AND ALLOWS THEIR ENTIRE DAILY SCHEDULE TO BE DICTATED BY ANOTHER PERSON, THEY MAY ALREADY BE IN A MANIPULATIVE DEPENDENCY. ON TOP OF THAT, EVEN WHEN AT WORK OR ELSEWHERE, THE PERSON IS PERPETUALLY CONTROLLED THROUGH MESSAGES, CALLS, AND REPROACHES. THIS RELENTLESS OVERWHELM IS A KEY REASON PEOPLE REMAIN IN THE GROUP FOR SO LONG — THEY SIMPLY NEVER GET A CHANCE TO REFLECT OR DOUBT, BECAUSE THEY'RE ALWAYS BUSY FULFILLING SOMETHING.

4.2 HIERARCHY AND POWER STRUCTURES

Absolute Authority of the Leader

Maria presented herself as the direct successor of divine powers, a sort of reborn Mary Magdalene, meant to guide us on the path to God. She placed herself above all laws and morals; we were supposedly eternally indebted to her. Any doubt about her authority was portrayed as satanic confusion.

Clear Ranking System and Control Over Members

A close circle of followers held privileged status, while others had to "prove themselves." This fostered competition, obedience, and a drive to meet her divine standards. I was convinced of her divine mission and the so-called "healing center" — a project she described in glowing terms but never actually realized. It was supposed to be something like a health and rescue hub. For years, I invested in this idea and even modified my career plans by joining emergency services so I could one day "do good" there. The center, where sick people would purportedly find healing through her divine power, remained nothing more than a phantom — a promise that motivated me and many others without ever becoming a reality.

Harsh Disciplinary Measures

Any deviation from Maria's rules was met with punishment — insults, violence, or the withdrawal of basic necessities. Personal belongings were destroyed as a means of coercion, and all forms of criticism were immediately silenced. It became clear to me that disobedience would inevitably lead to pain. Any attempt to question her divine mandate carried the looming threat of both physical and psychological consequences

Control of Communication and Isolation

Conversations with outsiders were strictly monitored, and family and friends were deemed dangerous influences. Speaking critically about the sect meant risking punishment. Over time, I grew increasingly isolated, losing trust in anyone outside Maria's circle.

She redirected my focus toward what she called "evidence" that the world was ruled by Lucifer — an elaborate web of satanic secret societies and corrupt politicians who, she claimed, abused children and manipulated global events. These dark narratives smothered my ability to trust others, instilling a deep, paralyzing fear of the outside world.

Subchapter in Brief

A STRICT HIERARCHY, AUTHORITARIAN LEADERSHIP, AND BRUTAL PUNISHMENTS ENSURED THAT MARIA'S AUTHORITY WAS NEVER QUESTIONED. FOR ANYONE OBSERVING A SIMILAR DYNAMIC — SEEING A PERSON WHO BLINDLY SUBMITS TO A SINGLE FIGURE, ACCEPTS VIOLENCE, AND NO LONGER RECOGNIZES ANY ALTERNATIVES — THIS SHOULD BE A WARNING SIGN. IT ALSO EXPLAINS WHY A SECT MEMBER WILL OFTEN STAY FOR A LONG TIME: THE IDEA OF LOSING THE SEEMINGLY GOD-ORDAINED LEADER — THE ONE WHO SHOWS THE WAY TO GOD AND KEEPS THE OUTSIDE WORLD'S HORRORS AT BAY — SEEMS WORSE THAN ENDURING THE FAMILIAR CONFINES OF THE SECT.

4.3 MANIPULATION TECHNIQUES

Emotional Overwhelm (Love Bombing)

New members were initially showered with praise and intense attention, creating a strong sense of dependence. I, too, continuously received messages from Maria praising my progress and emphasizing how vital I was to her divine mission. This constant reinforcement initially boosted my ego, but eventually, it dulled my ability to accept criticism.

Social Isolation and Fearmongering

Family and friends were portrayed as dangerous influences, obstacles to my "spiritual growth." Maria claimed the world outside was ruled by Lucifer. Again and again, I was shown videos of horrific crimes, secret conspiracies, satanic circles, child abuse, and other disturbing acts committed by strangers. This relentless flood of shocking content kept me in a state of constant paranoia. My fear of the outside world became so overwhelming that I eventually believed only Maria could protect me. With my mind trapped in permanent crisis mode, there was no mental space left to question her authority.

Thought Control and Mystical Elevation

Critical thinking was condemned as negative energy. Maria claimed to possess clairvoyant abilities, to receive divine messages, and to be in direct contact with God. I became convinced that she was Mary Magdalene and that she alone knew what God expected of me. My entire thought process revolved around her instructions. Any external media or literature was dismissed as manipulative propaganda from evil forces, steadily narrowing my world until it revolved solely around her.

Selective Information and Behavioral Control

Only Maria's knowledge mattered. Every aspect of daily life was tightly regulated — from what we ate to how we spent our free time. Excursions into the "normal" world were deemed dangerous and corrupting. Instead of critically evaluating my situation, I absorbed her messages and watched endless videos of terrifying scenarios. Rather than recognizing the abuse happening within the sect, my mind was consumed by fear — fear of the outside world, of its supposed evils, of everything beyond Maria's control.

Subchapter in Brief

THE SECT EMPLOYED A WIDE RANGE OF MANIPULATION TECHNIQUES. IF YOU NOTICE THAT A LOVED ONE RELIES ON A SINGLE SOURCE OF "TRUTH," BECOMES ISOLATED, AND DEVELOPS INTENSE PANIC, IT'S TIME TO PAY CLOSE ATTENTION. WHY DO PEOPLE STAY SO LONG? BECAUSE THEY BELIEVE THAT WITHOUT THIS SPIRITUAL GUIDANCE, THEY WOULD BE COMPLETELY EXPOSED TO THE DARK FORCES OUT-SIDE. THE INTERNAL PRESSURE, FEAR, AND PARANOIA BECOME SO OVERWHELMING THAT THE SECT'S APPARENT SAFETY, EVEN WITH ITS ABUSES, FEELS LIKE THE LESSER EVIL.

4.4 CHANGES IN RELATIONSHIPS WITH FAMILY AND FRIENDS

Reduced Contact and Growing Conflicts

Because of the relentless focus on childhood wounds and the supposed guilt my parents bore for my unhappiness, a chronic tension developed. I withdrew from my family — out of shame, fear, or the belief that they would never understand my path. My parents stood there, bewildered by my barrage of accusations, while I remained acutely aware that Maria scrutinized my every move and would hold me accountable.

Estrangement and Distorted Perception

The outside world was cast as dangerous and ignorant. I believed that only within the sect could I attain genuine insight. Friends and family became obstacles to my spiritual growth. Even professionally, I aligned myself with Maria's directives. I joined the emergency medical services, believing it was a stepping stone toward working in the healing center she envisioned — a facility she claimed was ordained by God. Anything outside this divine plan seemed pointless, even threatening.

Emotional Isolation and Guilt

I avoided social gatherings, ashamed of my circumstances and fearful of how others might react. Maria monitored all communication, demanding to know exactly what I had shared. Expressing any criticism externally was strictly forbidden. Under constant scrutiny and the ever-present weight of guilt, I felt like a failure — like someone who was hindering Maria's holy mission. That thought alone became unbearable.

Subchapter in Brief

THE SECT ACTIVELY ENCOURAGED ISOLATION FROM FAMILY AND FRIENDS. IF CLOSE RELATIONSHIPS SUDDENLY GET LABELED AS "TOXIC," IT'S TIME TO BE CAUTIOUS. FROM A SECT MEMBER'S PERSPECTIVE, YOU STAY SO LONG BECAUSE YOU BELIEVE YOUR OWN DOUBTS OR YOUR FAMILY'S CRITICISM ENDANGER THE DIVINE MISSION. THERE IS A FEAR THAT YOU ARE LOST WITHOUT THE SECT.

4.5 PERSONAL FEELINGS AND THOUGHTS DURING MY TIME IN THE SECT

Doubts and Subtle Realizations

There were moments when I noticed contradictions: Why were Maria's prophecies never fulfilled? Why was the promised center never built? Why did she claim to suffer from incurable illnesses supposedly caused by my "inner issues," yet no clear diagnosis was ever made? But I had no space to pursue these doubts. I was constantly occupied with tasks, crises, threats, and new horror stories about the evil world. Instead of questioning, I focused on fulfilling her demands so as not to interfere with her divine purpose.

Sense of Belonging and Fear of Punishment

I also felt a sense of belonging: my spiritual questions were acknowledged, I received praise, and I was commended for my progress. The price I paid was the constant fear of punishment. This mix of emotional warmth and intense intimidation kept me trapped.

Emotional Isolation and Brief Moments of Clarity

Occasionally, I recognized the violence, the illogic, the exploitation with stark clarity. But I was alone. The outside world seemed toxic, and the sect was my only point of reference. Who would help me if I left when everything outside was supposedly dangerous, as Maria insisted? My distorted perception and fear kept me in check.

Subchapter in Brief

INSIDE, I WAS TORN BETWEEN DOUBT, HOPE, A SENSE OF BELONG-
ING, AND FEAR. THIS INNER TURMOIL WAS CRUCIAL: YOU STAY IN
THE SECT BECAUSE YOU BELIEVE YOU CANNOT SURVIVE OUTSIDE IT.
WHILE YOU SUFFER ON THE INSIDE, YOU STILL FEEL THAT YOU'RE
SERVING A DIVINE PLAN.

ADDITIONAL INSIGHT AND DAILY ROUTINE: WHY YOU STAY IN A SECT FOR SO LONG

To fully understand why I remained in the sect for so long, it's crucial to grasp the psychological dynamics at play. In a group like this, a perpetual state of emergency prevails — every moment is dominated by Maria's control, her teachings looming over everything.

Constant Overwhelm and Uncertainty

With endless tasks, sudden phone calls — often during work hours, requiring my immediate response — and the exhaustive monitoring of my time, I lived in a state of relentless stress. There was never a chance to pause, reflect, or critically evaluate my situation. There was always some "urgent" crisis — a betrayal, a conflict, or a new divine revelation that demanded my immediate attention. The cycle never stopped.

Deeply Rooted Belief

I was utterly convinced that Maria had been sent by God — perhaps even a reincarnation of Mary Magdalene. This belief shaped my entire perception of her power, her mood swings, and her demands. Doubting her felt like doubting God. Leaving her would have meant dismantling my entire worldview — an unthinkable act at the time.

Meaning Through an Alleged Life Mission

Maria convinced me that I was part of her divine plan, that I had a crucial role to play in fulfilling it. The proposed healing center — a place for spiritual and "health" services that never materialized — became my purpose. From that moment on, I viewed my job, my decisions, and my entire life only through the lens of serving Maria's divine mission. As a result, doubting her meant doubting my own life's meaning.

Manipulation Through Fear of the Outside World

By making me watch countless videos and read numerous reports on abuse, satanic groups, political conspiracies, depraved practices, and moral degeneracy, she shattered my trust in society at large. Paranoia took hold — I trusted no one and saw Lucifer's influence everywhere. This relentless psychological bombardment made me so deeply suspicious that, despite its oppressive nature, the sect felt like the only safe haven.

No External Support System

By then, I had lost contact with my family and friends. Without any reliable outside relationships, I became entirely dependent on the sect for any sense of social connection. Even though Maria's approval was manipulative and conditional, it still felt preferable to what I had been led to believe was the cold and dangerous "outside" world.

These factors combined explain why people remain in sects despite obvious abuses. It's not a matter of ignorance or foolishness but a complex mix of psychological pressure, instilled fear, manipulated purpose, loss of identity, relentless overwork, and emotional dependence.

DAILY ROUTINE

Between Digital Highs and Destructive Routine

08:00 - 09:00: The Morning as the Signal to Begin Isolation
In the sparse apartment, the day begins almost mechanically:

- 08:00 - 08:20:
  Through headphones, the member listens to the meticulously rehearsed address of the cult leader. Her voice declares, "I love you – I am the truth!" The mantra is repeated over and over. This audio serves as the only anchor in the otherwise desolate silence, focusing the mind on absolute authority — even though the connection is purely digital.

- 08:20 - 08:30:
  In the dim light, a personal prayer to God follows:
  "I am a bad person, please help me!" These words are not just an admission but a ritual — one that begins the day with deep self-contempt.

- 08:30 - 09:00:
  Guided meditation leads the member deeper into the "truth" as prescribed by the cult leader. With each passing moment, the oppressive weight of the day ahead becomes more tangible — an endless cycle of meaningless tasks, each obligation chasing the next.

09:00 - 11:00: Digital Self-Discipline and the Endless Stream of Orders
The morning is devoted entirely to organization — and relentless self-criticism:

- 09:00 – 10:00:
  In the plain-text chat, the only means of group communication, daily tasks are coordinated. Members scrutinize each other's shortcomings. *For example:*
  > "Did you see that Thomas submitted the shopping list too late again? He is harming our mission!"

  Constant comparisons are drawn between what is "good" and what is "bad," with every personal failure amplified and dissected.

- 10:00 – 11:00:
  Today's meals are planned. The member compiles a shopping list of organic, sugar-free ingredients. Meanwhile, new messages flood in, announcing fresh procedures or directives from the cult leader.
  For example:
  > "New instruction: From now on, only vegan ready-made products without added sugar — any mistake endangers everyone's success!"

The constant flow of information forces the mind to rush from one pointless task to the next — never allowing a moment of respite.

11:00 - 13:00: The Only Phone Call Sparks Euphoria & Humiliation
Sometimes, the cult leader calls in the morning; sometimes, she does not.
When she does, it becomes the highlight of the day:

- 11:00 – 11:15:
  The moment the phone rings, the member experiences a brief but
  intense euphoria — the only direct human contact in an otherwise
  digital existence.

- 11:15 – 12:45:
  But the conversation quickly descends into relentless humiliation. The
  cult leader bombards the member with accusations such as:
  > "You are to blame for my illness. You are incapable of
  > disciplining yourself. Your failure burdens me every day!"
  **Approximately 80% of the call is consumed by these harsh, personal
  attacks that erode the member's self-esteem. Once the call ends,
  the member is left with a profound sense of emptiness and ongoing
  self-criticism.**

- 12:45 – 13:00:
  After the call, the member reflects on the conversation, takes notes,
  and records any newly gained "insights" or revelations with supposed
  clarity.

13:00 - 16:00: Grocery Runs

The afternoon offers brief excursions outside the apartment, yet even here, digital control remains absolute:

- 13:00 – 15:00:

  The member embarks on multiple grocery runs to various organic markets. Along the way, digital messages serve as constant reminders of past oversights. *For example:*

  > *"Those who shop carelessly weaken the mission — check every item for hidden sugar and take every detail seriously! You do want to become a better person!"*

  Covering the cost of these trips is considered an act of devotion. At the destination, no package is simply left at the door — bags may only be set down once the cult leader grants permission. Until then, the member remains in the car, ever ready to follow instructions at a moment's notice.

- 15:00 – 16:00:

  Back in the apartment, while working alone in the kitchen, the member receives further messages with new instructions. Every action becomes a test of loyalty and discipline.

If no grocery run is scheduled, the member instead prepares two meals for the cult leader and delivers them.

16:00 - 18:00: Chaotic Chat Discussions
The remainder of the afternoon is marked by intense, ongoing chat discussions across various groups:

Reflection Group
Here, members relentlessly debate the mistakes of others while being constantly reminded that they are no better themselves.
For example:
> "Maria emphasized again today that you are too narcissistic and lazy — your behavior is harming the entire group!"

Information Group
This group serves as a channel for the leader's latest decisions, new procedures, and organizational changes. Each new command abruptly disrupts the member's train of thought, forcing them to shift focus to the next meaningless task.

Project Group – Furniture Cleaning
In this strictly controlled group, a select few devote themselves meticulously to cleaning seating areas. Every fresh cleaning cloth becomes a symbol of devotion, and no speck of dirt goes unnoticed.

Personal Development Group
Here, members confess their daily progress along with even the smallest transgressions. Nothing escapes the leader's scrutiny, leading to incessant self-flagellation. Trapped in an endless cycle of confessions, they chase an unattainable standard of perfection.

18:00 - 20:00: : Flood of Information and Work Tasks
The evening brings a paradoxical mix of digital manipulation and additional work assignments:

- 18:00 – 18:30:
  World Info Group
  Here, members read the latest posts on conspiracy theories — ranging from the flat Earth to the Illuminati and other mysterious forces.

  > For example:
  > "The world is an illusion, controlled by Lucifer!
  > The Illuminati are his subjects — whoever fails to
  > recognize this will burn in hell!"

  Experience Group
  In this separate group, grim reports circulate, recounting how deeply religious individuals have "advanced" under the cult leader's guidance. The reports also describe the perverse fantasies and psychological breakdowns observed in other members. These stories are profoundly unsettling, further deepening the members' sense of isolation.

- 18:30 – 20:00:
  Specific Work Tasks
  Each member is assigned additional tasks, such as online research, running errands around the city, or cleaning the cult's apartment — always requiring the cult leader's explicit permission.

20:00 - 22:00: Destructive Leisure and Humiliation

During this time, the member is supposed to "relax," yet the digital world offers no respite:

- 20:00 – 21:00:

  Another ritualized cooking session takes place — alone in the kitchen, accompanied by digital reminders of personal failure.

- 21:00 – 22:00:

  The evening culminates in a particularly destructive chat group that every member is required to read daily:

  Humiliation Group

  Here, the cult leader personally and unambiguously condemns each member, portraying them as narcissistic, greedy, power-obsessed, envious, and arrogant.

  > For example:
  > "You are all failures — your ego, your greed, and your arrogance destroy me every day. Only those who discipline themselves might ever achieve anything! You are the worst!"

  These relentless messages erode the member's self-image, leaving no space for positive thoughts.

22:00 - 24:00: Evening Ritual

The final rite moves from self-reproach to apparent grace:

- 22:00 – 23:00:
  Self-Reflection on Personal Weaknesses
  During this hour, the member must focus on a predetermined personal flaw — whether it be alleged greed, narcissistic tendencies, or ingratitude toward the cult leader, Maria. As part of the ritual, they must document in writing why this trait developed and how it harms both the mission and the leader. Every minute revolves around the same relentless question: How deep do my faults truly run?

- 23:00 – 23:30:
  Declaration of Love to the Cult Leader
  Next, the member turns inward, cultivating a sense of deep affection and devotion toward Maria. For half an hour, every thought centers on the mantra:
  "She is my salvation — I am nothing without her."
  What appears to be an act of devotion only serves to further erode the self.

- 23:30 – 24:00:
  Bible Reading and Concluding Prayer
  The only permitted reading — the Bible — is now studied. The member reads devoutly selected passages, pre-approved by Maria. Immediately afterward, they offer a final prayer to God, asking for forgiveness and inner cleansing. Only after this final declaration of humility is the member allowed to sleep.

Chapter in Brief

LIFE IN THE SECT FOLLOWED A STRICT SYSTEM: RITUALS, A RIGID
HIERARCHY, PSYCHOLOGICAL AND PHYSICAL VIOLENCE, EMOTIONAL
MANIPULATION, GRADUAL ISOLATION FROM THE OUTSIDE WORLD,
AND A DAILY ROUTINE DRIVEN BY FEAR AND CONSPIRACY THEO-
RIES. TOTAL CONTROL OVER ONE'S TIME, THOUGHTS, FEELINGS, AND
SOCIAL CONTACTS LED TO COMPLETE DEPENDENCY ON THE SECT
LEADER. DESPITE GROWING INTERNAL DOUBTS, I STAYED FOR A
LONG TIME BECAUSE MY ENTIRE SYSTEM OF BELIEFS AND VALUES, MY
CAREER PATH, AND MY WORLDVIEW WERE INSEPARABLE FROM HER
TEACHINGS. I FEARED THE THREATENING OUTSIDE WORLD, BELIEVED
IN HER DIVINE MISSION, AND HAD NO MENTAL SPACE LEFT TO QUES-
TION MYSELF CRITICALLY.

WHAT FAMILY MEMBERS CAN DO

For family members and outsiders, these descriptions offer valuable insights into recognizing potential warning signs: increasing isolation, rigid rituals, unquestioned authority, fear of criticism, financial exploitation, and the feeling that one cannot exist without the group are clear red flags. If you notice these patterns, respond with sensitivity, try to engage in conversation, and seek professional help if needed. Only through understanding, patience, and empathy can you help someone escape this kind of psychological captivity.

.

Chapter Five

LOVE AS A LIFELINE

5.1 MEETING MY FUTURE WIFE – A NEW CONNECTION INSTEAD OF CONTROL

During my time in the cult, I lived in a constant state of emotional constriction and fear. Bound by rigid regulations, spiritual rules, and the perpetual feeling of never quite measuring up, my world felt small, gray, and suffocating. Then, in the midst of this isolation, I met Valentina — a self-confident, independent woman unlike anyone I had ever encountered. She was committed, proactive, and self-assured, but above all, she was free. Her very presence stood in stark contrast to the cult members, who were always shadowed by suspicious glances and manipulative words.

Our first encounter happened while working in emergency medical services, where we were both employed. For me, the job had long since become routine — shift work, emergency calls, deployments — without much human connection. But that changed with Valentina. During our twelve-hour shifts, we had time to talk, to swap personal stories, to share laughter. Where human emotion in the cult was met with harsh judgment, Valentina offered a natural warmth. Instead of the strict silence and constant scrutiny I was accustomed to, I finally experienced something that felt light and easy.

But I want to make one thing clear: despite how it may sound, I didn't just meet someone, fall in love, and immediately leave the cult. It wasn't that simple. In reality, it took about a year and a half before I finally managed to break away. That time was filled with inner conflict, relapses into old patterns, and a constant internal tug-of-war.

From the very beginning, Maria tried to control my budding relationship with Valentina. She claimed that God had told her Valentina wasn't the right woman for me, that my true partner had yet to come. But first, she said, Valentina could serve as a kind of "transitional girlfriend" — if she met certain conditions.

These conditions included working through any past relationship wounds and keeping a detailed journal of the process. I, in turn, was expected to monitor her progress. According to Maria, Valentina was supposedly "controlled by Lucifer" and could only be freed from his influence by analyzing her past.

I passed these absurd demands on to Valentina, carefully avoiding any mention of the cult. But she saw through it immediately — she knew these bizarre requirements weren't coming from me alone. She sensed that someone in the background was pulling the strings. Though she didn't yet know about Maria or the extent of her influence, she could feel the presence of a manipulative force. Frustrated and angry over the pressure she was being put under, Valentina once smashed a trash can in front of friends (when I wasn't there) just to vent. But instead of walking away, she chose to play along. She worked through her past, complied with the demand — not because she believed in it, but because she wanted to give me some breathing room.

That doesn't mean she was fine with it. Far from it. She endured a lot — more than she should have. She was often disappointed when I suddenly disappeared because the cult demanded something of me. I was torn between two worlds, unable to commit fully to either. For a long time, I remained caught in the struggle, afraid to break free but unable to let go of the glimpse of freedom she had shown me.

WHAT FAMILY MEMBERS CAN DO

If you see your loved one opening up to a new, caring partner, it doesn't necessarily mean everything will suddenly get better. Even with the arrival of a supportive relationship from the outside, the cult's influence remains. Leaving can be a lengthy journey marked by relapses. The new partner also has to hold on through this process and will often become a target of manipulation and tests. The struggle for freedom is tough, and it's not uncommon for the cult to try to undermine this new bond.

5.2 GROWING AWARENESS AND SELF-REFLECTION— COMPARISON OPENS YOUR EYES

Through my time with Valentina, I began making comparisons that had once been impossible for me. She wasn't just empathetic — she was truly hands-on. She worked in emergency services, actively helped others, never complained about her burdens, and tackled challenges head-on. Her energy and practical compassion stood in stark contrast to the cult, which constantly spoke of grand spiritual missions but offered little in the way of real, tangible help.

While Maria relied on endless words and elaborate teachings, Valentina was out in the real world — acting instead of merely preaching.

Still, I was far from free. Again and again, I was summoned to cult meetings, leaving Valentina disappointed as I failed to summon the courage to fully break away. These backslides weighed on both of us. She had to watch me walk away whenever the cult called, and each time, it hurt her. I felt trapped — pulled between two worlds.

And yet, my awareness of the cult's absurdity kept growing. More and more, I questioned everything: Why the rigid dietary rules? The constant accusations? The relentless fearmongering? Why should my life be governed by endless justifications and the fear of punishment, when what I experienced with Valentina was so beautiful, honest, and liberating?

Life is short. And with every passing day, I saw more clearly how pointless it was to spend it in perpetual submission and fear.

WHAT FAMILY MEMBERS CAN DO

If someone close to you is torn, it doesn't mean your support is ineffective.

Realizing there are alternatives to the cult often happens gradually. Be

patient. Even though there may be setbacks and disappointments, remain

understanding. Every moment of self-reflection is an important step.

5.3 REACTIONS OF FAMILY AND FRIENDS – RENEWED CLOSENESS INSTEAD OF ISOLATION

As I changed internally, my relationships with others changed as well. My family noticed that I was no longer so closed off. I showed interest, laughed with them, and visited more often. Thanks to Valentina's positive influence, my mother began to hope that I might still break free from the cult.

Friends and colleagues saw I was becoming more relaxed and accessible. Despite my relapses and the moments when I was dragged back into the cult's influence, I increasingly showed that there was another person inside me — someone who could laugh, empathize, and act independently. Even Valentina, who suffered herself and sometimes snapped from anger — like the day she smashed the trash can — remained in my life and supported me. She knew that my behavior wasn't solely my own but also heavily influenced by outside forces.

The rekindling of family ties and acceptance by friends gave me strength. They showed me that there was a social safety net waiting to catch me if I fell. At the same time, I realized how determined the cult would be to weaken these renewed old contacts and keep me from growing closer to my family. The more evident it became that I was on the path to change, the tighter the cult clung to me.

WHAT FAMILY MEMBERS CAN DO

Take advantage of any positive changes to carefully build bridges. Don't overwhelm your loved one with demands; show understanding and confidence. Acknowledge how hard it is to fight this inner battle — both for the affected individual and for a new partner who must endure the situation in the background, unable to force immediate change.

5.4 A BROKEN SHOULDER AS A TURNING POINT – PHYSICAL INJURY REVEALS THE TRUTH

A fateful accident finally unmasked the cult's true face. On a ski trip with Valentina — her special birthday gift to me — I took a bad fall and broke my shoulder. Suddenly, I needed help. Valentina didn't hesitate: she was there for me, helping me dress, cook, and manage my medication. She stood by me, even though I had repeatedly disappointed her in the past by going back to the cult.

The cult, however, reacted with indifference and coldness. No get-well wishes, no compassion — just more demands and accusations. It didn't matter that I was injured; I was expected to continue fulfilling my "duties." This lack of empathy underscored how little I mattered to them as a person. The contrast between Valentina's genuine care and the cult's emotional coldness became strikingly clear.

External influences intensified my internal shift. A sentence I heard in a seminar outside the cult — "Jesus has already paid for all our sins" — contradicted the endless blame the cult leader placed on us. A therapist asked me outright if I was in a cult. Such frank words and an outside perspective finally shattered the carefully constructed illusion. My broken shoulder represented not just a physical injury but also an internal break I could no longer ignore.

It had taken 1.5 years from my first encounters with Valentina to reach this point, where I slowly realized I had to leave.

Her patience, her perseverance, and her willingness to comply with even bizarre demands — like keeping a journal of her past relationships — to give me breathing space had ultimately helped me to gradually wake up. Despite her own wounds and the emotional strain caused by my indecision, Valentina stayed by my side out of love and compassion.

WHAT FAMILY MEMBERS CAN DO

This story shows that even a new, positive relationship does not instantly lead someone out of a cult. The process is often long, painful, and accompanied by setbacks. The cult will do everything it can to undermine the new influence. Yet a patient, loving individual who can handle disappointment can become a decisive lifeline.

Chapter in Brief

MEETING VALENTINA SHOWED ME WHAT IT FEELS LIKE TO BE GENU-
INELY LOVED, RESPECTED, AND SUPPORTED — WITHOUT CONDITIONS
AND WITHOUT LIES. BUT THIS WAS NO QUICK OR STRAIGHTFOR-
WARD PATH OUT OF THE CULT. IT TOOK ME A TOTAL OF 1.5 YEARS TO
FIND THE COURAGE TO TRULY LEAVE. DURING THAT TIME, I WAS IN-
WARDLY TORN AND KEPT RETURNING TO FULFILL THE CULT LEADER'S
WISHES. VALENTINA HAD TO PUT UP WITH A LOT: ENDURE DISAP-
POINTMENTS AND PASS RIDICULOUS TESTS INDIRECTLY IMPOSED ON
HER BY THE CULT. SHE HAD TO WATCH ME RUN BACK EVERY TIME THE
CULT CALLED, YET SHE NEVER GAVE UP.

FAMILY AND FRIENDS WELCOMED MY NEW OPENNESS, BUT THESE
RENEWED BONDS ALSO DIDN'T HAPPEN OVERNIGHT. THE EXPERIENCE
OF BREAKING MY SHOULDER, THE CULT'S LACK OF EMPATHY, AND
VALENTINA'S UNCONDITIONAL SUPPORT MADE IT PAINFULLY CLEAR
THAT I HAD TO FREE MYSELF. LOVE BECAME MY LIFELINE, BUT THAT
LIFELINE HAD TO WITHSTAND POWERFUL UNDERTOWS. IT WASN'T
UNTIL THE COMBINATION OF EMOTIONAL CLOSENESS, CRITICAL EX-
TERNAL EXPERIENCES, AND MY OWN REFLECTION THAT I WAS ABLE
TO MAKE A FINAL BREAK.

WHAT FAMILY MEMBERS CAN DO

The message of this chapter is unmistakable: a new, loving relationship can be a key factor on the path out of a cult, but it does not guarantee quick success. The cult will try to sabotage this new bond, and setbacks are likely. As family members, you should remain patient, offer support, and avoid judgment. Recognize that the internal struggle for the person involved is complex and that the new partner has to tolerate a lot before an exit can succeed. Good help is rare, but perseverance, understanding, and compassion can make all the difference.

Chapter Six

THE REALIZATION

6.1 THE MOMENT OF CLARITY

It was a quiet, cool evening when I sat with Valentina in her apartment. The living room was bathed in warm light, wrapping me in a sense of safety I hadn't felt in years. For the first time in a long while, I felt seen.

Doubts had been building inside me for weeks — small cracks in the carefully constructed illusion of my so-called "spiritual community." Until recently, I would never have dared to voice these thoughts aloud. But something was different that night. Maybe it was the understanding look in Valentina's eyes, or perhaps it was the lingering weight of my last video call with my family, which had shaken me more than I wanted to admit.

During that call, my parents had looked at me with raw, unfiltered concern. Their eyes were wet with tears, their voices trembled, and their questions were so direct that I could no longer evade them. For the first time in years, I saw my life through their eyes. The rules, the pressure, the relentless fear that governed my every move — suddenly, it all seemed so foreign, so wrong.

Even before I found the words, I knew what I was about to say. My throat tightened, my heart pounded. Yet I realized I had to say it.

"Am I in a cult?"

My voice was low, barely more than a whisper, and on the verge of breaking. The question hung in the air like a lead weight. The silence that followed seemed to shift the entire room.

Valentina held my gaze, steady and unwavering. Her eyes brimmed with understanding and relief, as though she had been waiting for me to arrive at this moment. There was no judgment in her expression — only deep compassion and the faintest smile, one that seemed to say: "At last, you're saying it."

With that single sentence, I unlocked a door that had been sealed shut for far too long. A flood of emotions crashed over me — shock, anger, sadness, relief, fear — everything at once. I remembered the messages where cult members had called me a "servant," the humiliations, the threats, the constant surveillance.

There was no going back now. The illusion of safety had shattered.

But in the midst of it all, a faint spark of hope flickered. For the first time, I had broken free from my inner paralysis.

6.2 THE REALITY SINKS IN

Realizing I was in a cult was not only painful but terrifying. This was no harmless group of spiritual seekers — it was a system of control, emotional abuse, and the constant threat of violence. For years, the cult leader had dictated every aspect of our lives, keeping us in check with the ever-present fear of demons, Lucifer, or other dark forces. These imaginary enemies had been planted so deeply into our thoughts that even in the most ordinary situations, we felt under siege.

I remembered members who had been physically punished or publicly humiliated for "disobedience." Hints about the consequences of leaving were clear — slander, attacks on my social circle, maybe even physical retaliation. Surveillance was constant. My apartment was no sanctuary; others had access to my keys, furniture was moved, small, deliberate signs were left behind — a silent message: "We see everything. We control you."

This reality was shocking, yet it also brought clarity. I finally understood why I had hesitated for so long. The exhaustion, the fear, the mental fog — all of it served a purpose: total submission. But now, I was beginning to see the full picture. And once I did, I knew what had to come next.

I refused to be intimidated any longer.

6.3 PREPARING TO LEAVE

Now that I understood my predicament, it was time to act. But leaving impulsively would be dangerous. Without a solid plan, I would be vulnerable to retaliation, manipulation, or even being lured back in. So I started my escape step by step.

The first priority was finding a new apartment — one far from the cult's reach. I was willing to pay higher rent just to put distance between myself and their control. Every day counted. I spent hours searching real estate websites until I found a place that felt safe. Within days, I signed a lease. It was my first real, tangible step toward freedom. The knowledge that I would soon have my own, untouchable space filled me with a renewed sense of strength.

At the same time, I contacted a lawyer to serve as a buffer between me and the cult leader. This would protect me from direct threats. His role was to draft cease-and-desist letters, establish legal protections, and set firm boundaries. I also minimized my digital footprint — getting a new phone number and preparing to sever all ties.

A call to a national cult hotline (Sektenhotline) confirmed what I already knew: I had been the victim of a highly manipulative group. The counselors listened patiently, urged me to act quickly, and most importantly, told me not to blame myself.

"You're not naive," they assured me. "You've been systematically conditioned for years. But the fact that you're taking steps to leave — that's an act of courage."

Their words gave me confidence. So did Valentina, who stood by me relentlessly. She took my fears seriously, reminded me of my strength, and pushed me forward whenever my doubts threatened to pull me back.

Together, we planned what we called a "lightning move." Everything would happen in a single day — quick, precise, and efficient, with the help of trusted friends and colleagues. Within hours, I would be gone.

I ordered moving boxes, rented a van, and gathered people who could help at a moment's notice. Meanwhile, I worked with my lawyer to handle the formalities, ensuring I could avoid any direct confrontation.

6.4 FINAL DAYS IN THE CULT

The last few days felt like walking on thin ice. I had to pretend everything was normal to avoid suspicion. Any sign that I was planning to leave could bring retaliation — or worse, an attempt to pull me back in.

Ironically, my final task within the group was a handyman job. I had been assigned to sand down garden furniture with another member. With my injured shoulder, the work was grueling, but I played along, forcing myself to move slowly — not out of weakness, but to maintain the illusion that I was still compliant.

As we worked in tense silence, I could feel his unease. His eyes flicked repeatedly toward the door.

Something about his behavior struck me: he was nervous. It was almost as though he sensed something was wrong. Maybe, deep down, he knew what I was about to do.

And for the first time, it dawned on me — not everyone was staying willingly. Maybe they, too, were trapped in this web of fear and guilt.

Meanwhile, my preparations for escape continued in the background:

My Family

I informed my family openly about my decision. They responded with tears, but also tremendous relief. They promised to stand by me and help in any way they could. That unconditional love was a huge comfort.

Valentina's Parents

After I explained the danger to Valentina's parents, they were deeply concerned about their daughter. Even so, they took my situation seriously and supported the idea of involving the police.

The Police

At the police station, I filed a record of my situation so there would be evidence if anything happened. An officer strongly advised me to cut all ties: move to a new address, get a new phone number — disappear until the threat had passed.

The Lawyer

In a meeting with my lawyer, we secured the legal side. From the threatening messages and contemptuous remarks to the financial demands, he saw clear grounds for legal action. After I moved out, he would handle every interaction with the cult leader and fend off threats, preventing the cult from re-entering my life.

Chapter in Brief

COMING TO THE STARK REALIZATION THAT I WAS IN A CULT WAS A MASSIVE TURNING POINT. IT SHATTERED MY PREVIOUS WORLD-VIEW BUT ALSO OPENED THE DOOR TO A SELF-DETERMINED LIFE. THROUGH THE EMOTIONAL SUPPORT OF MY FAMILY AND VALENTINA, MY UNDERSTANDING OF THE ACTUAL DANGERS, AND THE CAREFUL PLANNING OF MY EXIT, I GAINED INCREASING CERTAINTY AND CLARITY. THE PRACTICAL STEPS — FROM FINDING A NEW APARTMENT TO SECURING LEGAL SUPPORT AND ORCHESTRATING A QUICK MOVE — SYMBOLIZED MY COURAGE AND NEWLY DISCOVERED FREEDOM.

WHAT FAMILY MEMBERS CAN DO

For those affected, the message is clear: recognizing the truth is the first step. Though painful, that moment can mark the beginning of a journey toward genuine independence, safety, and healing. What follows are concrete measures: seek professional advice, take legal action, and build a stable environment offering understanding, support, and compassion. Anyone walking this path has the potential to break free from the shackles of a cult — regaining their own voice, rediscovering self-confidence, and, ultimately, breathing freely once more.

Chapter Seven

THE EXIT

7.1 THE BLITZ MOVE –
PHYSICAL EXIT AND COMMUNAL SPIRIT

Morning had finally arrived — the day I would reclaim my freedom. Every detail of the move had been meticulously planned. In the early hours, I drove alone to my old apartment one last time, checking that no one from the cult had slipped in unnoticed. My heart pounded as I turned the key in the lock. To my relief, everything was just as I had left it, but the tension remained. I knew that today, I would make a definitive break from my past.

Shortly afterward, my helpers arrived — close friends, colleagues, my family, and of course, Valentina, who had stood by me all this time. They came with trucks, vans, and a readiness to get things done. Despite the early hour, the mood was strikingly positive, almost festive. It felt as though we were on a mission where everyone understood how much was at stake. While film music from The Avengers blared on the radio, Valentina laughed, "The rescue squad has arrived!"

Before getting started, I asked everyone into the living room. The space was chaotic: boxes and furniture everywhere, some of it belonging to the cult leader. It weighed on me, that uncomfortable sense of shame at the mess. But the time had come to speak the truth.

"I was in a cult, and today I'm leaving it."

A brief silence followed before one of my friends put a hand on my shoulder and said firmly, "We're here to help you." No accusations, no questions — just support.

Tears welled up in my eyes as I realized: I wasn't alone.

You could feel the team's energy. Everyone knew instinctively what to do. One group sorted through furniture and belongings, labeling what should come along or be thrown out. Others began dismantling large pieces, while still others coordinated the transport. Since my shoulder was injured, I took on more of a conductor role, giving directions, clarifying questions, and making sure everything went smoothly.

There were moments when I came across triggering items — like a massive XXL sofa where I'd experienced so many painful moments. Materially, it had value, but my supporters understood its deeper weight.

Valentina said softly, "A new beginning sometimes means parting with things that cause pain."

Her words hit home. I decided to get rid of that sofa and other burdensome items. With each piece that disappeared, it felt as if I were discarding a part of my past. These symbolic actions were powerful: it wasn't just about boxes and furniture, but about shedding emotional burdens I could finally let go of.

To prevent cult members from entering the apartment at will, we changed the locks on the doors and storage rooms, removed my name from the doorbell, and made everything look as though I had never lived there. Then, we packed the cult leader's belongings into a van and later dropped them off outside her home.

As we unloaded, we felt uneasy seeing her silhouette behind the window. But there was no confrontation. We quickly returned to our convoy to avoid any discussions — or worse.

After blocking all contact details for cult members on my phones and social media, I realized that for the first time in ages, I was free.

When we arrived at my new apartment, the place was already set up. My helpers had moved in furniture and boxes, making it bright, orderly, and peaceful.

Relief washed over me — like a warm, protective blanket for my soul.

This communal effort symbolized a breakthrough — a new life in genuine freedom.

7.2 THE CULT'S REACTIONS –
LEGAL PROTECTION AND CLEAR BOUNDARIES

Hardly had I completed the physical exit when the cult's expected reactions began. They tried reaching me by phone, messenger, and email, but their messages went nowhere since I had blocked them. Even my family received strange calls with dramatic stories about supposedly life-threatening situations — all transparent attempts to lure me back. My parents responded firmly, "Please contact our son directly. This is harassment." After a few such confrontations, the cult gave up. It was as though they were scratching at an invisible wall — built with legal tools and personal resolve — through which they could not pass.

My lawyer was already in the loop, prepared with documentation and evidence in case the cult took legal action. Sure enough, the cult leader hired a lawyer and brought forward absurd allegations. But we responded confidently, refuting each accusation point by point and issuing cease-and-desist orders. Each of these steps reinforced my sense of security. Their attempts at intimidation bounced right off; the clear boundaries I set were effective. Eventually, the cult had no choice but to accept all my demands and leave me alone.

This legal protection carried a profound symbolic weight: it demonstrated to me and other survivors that leaving doesn't have to be followed by endless repercussions or threats. With professional support, patience, and clear communication, you can protect yourself. Experiencing how I could assert my rights gave me a new, powerful self-confidence.

7.3 EMOTIONAL CHALLENGES –
HEALING AND INNER FREEDOM

After I physically left, the hardest part began: the emotional reckoning. My time in the cult had left deep marks that wouldn't vanish overnight. Quiet moments brought flashbacks of violence, humiliation, and powerlessness. Any sudden movement on the street made my heart race. Often, I wondered, "Am I really safe now? Could someone come back at any moment to harass me?"

These inner battles were agonizing. Nightmares jolted me awake in a cold sweat, and everyday events reminded me of past abuse. Instead of running from it, I decided to face it head-on. I turned to therapeutic strategies: reality checks helped me distinguish between real threats and my fears. Journaling organized my feelings, and I allowed myself to express sadness and anger openly. Being honest with myself was a critical step toward recovery.

My social network played a central role. Valentina listened patiently, never judging me when I cried or lashed out. My family and friends gave me the support I needed, encouraging me to talk about what had happened but never pushing me. We spent time together doing things that had nothing to do with my past — walks in nature, cozy movie nights, and laid-back get-togethers with my old coworkers. Little by little, a new sense of security emerged, reminding me I wasn't alone.

I also tackled my fears by discovering new hobbies and turning to sports as a release for all that pent-up energy. Running or biking offered me a sense of freedom and vitality. Meditation and yoga helped me focus on the present instead of sinking into painful memories. Consciously choosing to shape my own life gave me a sense of liberation. Gradually, I learned to accept my past without letting it define me.

Eventually, I realized I was no longer a victim but a survivor — a realization that filled me with a renewed sense of self-worth.

Chapter in Brief

LEAVING A CULT INVOLVES FAR MORE THAN SIMPLY CROSSING A
PHYSICAL THRESHOLD.

IT REQUIRES CAREFUL PLANNING OF A "BLITZ MOVE," LEGAL SAFE-
GUARDS AGAINST PERSISTENT ATTEMPTS AT CONTACT, AND ABOVE
ALL A LONG, OFTEN PAINFUL JOURNEY OF EMOTIONAL HEALING. THE
MOMENT I DECIDED TO DISCARD MY OLD SOFA BECAME A PERSONAL
SYMBOL OF LETTING GO. BY TAKING PROFESSIONAL LEGAL STEPS,
DRAWING FIRM BOUNDARIES, AND BLOCKING ALL CULT CONTACTS,
I DEMONSTRATED THAT A CLEAN BREAK IS POSSIBLE. FOR ANYONE
WALKING A SIMILAR PATH, THOROUGH PREPARATION IS ESSENTIAL.
LEGAL COUNSEL, A SOLID SOCIAL NETWORK, AND RELIABLE COM-
PANIONS CAN ENSURE A SAFE PHYSICAL EXIT. YET THE EMOTIONAL
WORK NEEDS TIME AND SPACE — FEELINGS SUCH AS FEAR, LONE-
LINESS, AND GRIEF ARE NORMAL COMPANIONS. TALKING TO THER-
APISTS, CONFIDING IN TRUSTED FRIENDS OR FAMILY, ENGAGING IN
SPORTS, OR EXPLORING CREATIVE HOBBIES CAN HELP YOU FIND NEW
MEANING IN LIFE AND BREAK FREE FROM THE CHAINS OF THE PAST.

WHAT FAMILY MEMBERS CAN DO

This chapter aims to encourage families of cult members and offer insights into the exit process. The path out is complex, requiring both practical steps and inner strength — but a self-determined, free, and fulfilling life after the cult is entirely possible. That message is at the heart of it all: where fear and control once dominated, there can be room for freedom, healing, and hope.

Chapter Eight

HEALING
AND
NEW BEGINNINGS

8.1 CONVERSATIONS AS A PATH TO PROCESSING

My post-cult life was defined by deep introspection into my emotions, memories, and wounds. Speaking openly about my past experiences turned out to be one of the most important steps in my healing process. At first, however, finding the right words and organizing my thoughts was difficult. I had spent so long suppressing doubts, fears, and guilt that in my newfound freedom, I often felt overwhelmed by my emotions.

From the outset, Valentina was a tremendous support. We spent countless hours talking — over cups of tea or on walks in the nearby park. I recall one evening when I confessed, "Sometimes, I still feel trapped, as if an invisible thread is holding me back." Gently taking my hand and gazing into my eyes, she said, "You're free now, and you have every right to feel whatever arises in you — hurt, anger, or uncertainty." Her simple, empathetic words were like a key unlocking a sealed door within me. For the first time in ages, I saw my emotions as valid. Valentina helped me acknowledge them instead of dismissing or denying them, as I had been taught in the cult.

I had similar discussions with my family. We met in my parents' garden, a place that once symbolized security but had become laden with tension due to my long absences and lack of communication. Initially, there was some strain in the air, which gradually lifted under the warm sunlight and the scent of freshly cut grass. My mother, her voice trembling, spoke of her fear and helplessness during my time in the cult. My father put a reassuring hand on my shoulder when I apologized for keeping him and the rest of the family in the dark for so long. "What matters is that you're here now," he said, his voice filled with relief. Though painful, the process of voicing our unspoken worries, accusations, and misunderstandings allowed old wounds to heal. We came to understand that I wasn't the only one who had suffered — each family member had endured their own anguish.

Reconnecting with old friends was also crucial. I hesitated at first to dial long-silent numbers on my phone. Would they still understand me after all I'd been through? Yet when I finally found the courage, most responded with surprise — and compassion. "We had no idea what was happening with you," one old friend said. "But it all makes sense now."

Those conversations were often intense on both sides. I apologized for my past behavior, explaining the inner pressures and manipulations I had faced. Most people accepted my apology, and together, we carefully rebuilt our friendships on new, more honest foundations. Movie nights or lengthy talks over a glass of wine helped fill the gaps that had formed.

Subchapter in Brief

THROUGH RESPECTFUL, OPEN CONVERSATIONS WITH VALENTI-
NA, MY FAMILY, AND MY OLD FRIENDS, I LEARNED TO VALIDATE MY
SUPPRESSED FEELINGS, CLEAR UP MISUNDERSTANDINGS, AND FIND
EMOTIONAL SUPPORT. THIS WILLINGNESS TO SHARE TURNED OUT TO
BE A POWERFUL TOOL FOR HEALING DEEP-ROOTED WOUNDS AND RE-
CLAIMING A SENSE OF CLOSENESS.

8.2 RETURNING TO EVERYDAY ACTIVITIES

Once I broke through my initial emotional barriers, I craved a life where I could decide for myself — where I could shape my own choices, free from imposed restrictions. This included my diet, which had been governed by the strict, dogmatic vegan rules of the cult. For six years, I had given up so much, never questioning whether that lifestyle truly suited me.

Now, I faced a simple but profound question: How did I truly want to eat and live?

I chose a deliberate new beginning — at the dinner table as well. Reclaiming my culinary freedom became a symbol of self-determination. Together with Valentina, I went to a steak restaurant — a step that would have been unthinkable just a short time ago. That first bite wasn't just about the taste of meat; it was the taste of freedom.

But this shift in my diet was about more than just food. It marked the end of rigid dictates and the start of my own choices. A whole world of new flavors and experiences opened up to me — international cuisine, bustling markets, evenings spent cooking with friends. Life became vibrant and diverse again, and with that diversity came joy and energy I hadn't felt in years.

An equally liberating experience was planning regular getaways and trips. In the cult, each day had been structured as though the outside world didn't exist. Now, I inhaled the freedom of new possibilities.

Valentina and I took weekend trips to the ocean, hiked through the mountains, felt the wind against our faces, and rediscovered something I had been missing for far too long: a connection to the real, living world.

One particularly unforgettable moment was a riding vacation — exploring wide-open landscapes on gentle, steady horses. The sweeping views, the rhythmic drumming of hooves, the scent of grass and woods — all of it helped me find my place again in the larger scheme of things.

At the same time, my social bonds were slowly knitting back together. Shared experiences — movie nights, concerts (including one unforgettable film music concert, for which I gifted Valentina VIP tickets), spontaneous barbecues, sports outings, and long, laughter-filled dinners — became the mosaic pieces of my new life. The everyday moments that the cult had dismissed as trivial or irrelevant proved to be precious treasures. They gave me stability. Happiness. And growing self-confidence.

Subchapter in Brief

BY TAKING BACK CONTROL OVER MY DIET, EXPLORING TRAVEL AND LEISURE ACTIVITIES, AND OPENING MYSELF TO SHARED EXPERIENCES WITH VALENTINA, FAMILY, AND FRIENDS, I RETURNED TO A LIFE DEFINED BY DIVERSITY, FREEDOM, AND JOY — RATHER THAN LIMITATIONS.

8.3 PROFESSIONAL STABILITY AND PERSONAL PROJECTS

Another cornerstone of my healing process was choosing to maintain continuity in my professional life. Although nearly everything else was being rearranged, I stayed in my familiar field of work as a paramedic. The routine, camaraderie, and meaningful nature of the job kept me grounded. I knew I was needed there and that my efforts could make a real difference for others.

One afternoon, while chatting with my colleague Thomas at the station, he gently hinted that he had noticed a change in me. "If you ever need to talk, I'm here," he said without pushing. That simple offer reassured me that I didn't have to explain everything. My coworkers were willing to give me space, and that quiet understanding was incredibly valuable at a time when I still felt quite unsteady inside.

At the same time, I began exploring new, creative outlets. Redecorating my apartment became a personal ritual — each chosen item, each picture on the wall, and each piece of furniture symbolized my autonomy. I also revisited old hobbies: photography, writing, and immersing myself in books about distant cultures.

Writing down my experiences proved particularly healing. At first, I simply jotted my thoughts into a notebook, trying to make sense of everything. But soon, I had an idea: what if I wrote a book? A book that could support others facing similar challenges, offering them hope for a fresh start.

My relationship with Valentina also deepened in trust. What we had endured together brought us closer, proving that we could depend on each other even in the hardest times.

One evening, beneath a clear, starry sky in the mountains, I found the courage to propose. My voice shook with nerves as I asked if she would spend the rest of our lives by my side.

Her radiant "Yes" filled me with a sense of certainty — that although our past had left its scars, it did not define us. Instead, it had taught us what truly matters: love, understanding, freedom, and the power of sharing our story openly.

Writing the book, connecting with other former cult members, and occasionally speaking with professional counselors helped me unravel the last lingering shadows of my time in the cult.

I came to recognize that healing is an active process — one that requires both courage and patience. Every small step — whether a heartfelt conversation, a thoughtfully chosen piece of décor, or an honest sentence in my manuscript — helped me break free from old patterns.

And so, piece by piece, I built a stable foundation upon which I could shape my future with confidence.

Subchapter in Brief

PROFESSIONAL RELIABILITY, PERSONAL GROWTH THROUGH CREA-
TIVE PROJECTS, ACTIVE REFLECTION ON MY PAST, AND THE DECISION
TO BUILD A LIFE WITH VALENTINA FORMED A STURDY CORNERSTONE
FOR MY NEW START. I LEARNED TO ACCEPT MY STORY AS PART OF
MY IDENTITY WITHOUT LETTING IT CONTROL ME. INSTEAD, I BEGAN
USING IT AS A RESOURCE FOR NEW GOALS, IDEAS, AND PURPOSE.

Chapter in Brief

MY HEALING AFTER LEAVING WAS A COMPLEX BUT LIBERATING JOUR-
NEY.

OPEN-HEARTED CONVERSATIONS WITH VALENTINA, MY FAMILY,
AND MY OLD FRIENDS HELPED ME WORK THROUGH LONG-STANDING
WOUNDS AND REASSESS MY EMOTIONS. RECLAIMING MY FREEDOM IN
DIET, LEISURE ACTIVITIES, AND SOCIAL LIFE GAVE ME A NEWFOUND
SENSE OF VITALITY AND AUTONOMY. STABILITY AT WORK AND NEW
CREATIVE PROJECTS PROVIDED STRUCTURE AND MEANING, WHILE
WRITING HELPED ME UNDERSTAND MY PAST AND DEVELOP FUTURE
PERSPECTIVES.

WHAT FAMILY MEMBERS CAN DO

For family members of people involved in cults — and for others in similar situations — the key message is not to shy away from honest conversations, to rekindle new or old connections, and to give yourself permission to enjoy everyday pleasures. A steady job or other meaningful pursuits can offer stability while writing down your own story or connecting with other survivors can open up new perspectives. Step by step, it's possible to build a self-determined, fulfilling life beyond manipulative structures — a life where healing is not only possible but tangible.

Chapter Nine

MESSAGE AND LESSONS

9.1 INSIGHTS FOR RELATIVES: PATIENCE, OPENNESS, AND UNDERSTANDING

Family and friendships as anchors

Even though cults attempt to undermine family and friendship structures, the deep emotional bond usually remains intact. Parents, siblings, longtime friends — each represents a part of the past that cannot simply be erased. These relationships serve as a living archive of shared memories, offering warmth, belonging, and identity.

During my own time in the cult, I often felt as though this new "community" was meant to replace any sense of familial closeness. The cult leader repeatedly insisted that the group was now my true family. Yet despite these attempts, my longing for my real family never disappeared.

One particular Christmas celebration they invited me to moved me more than I cared to admit. The scent of pine branches, the familiar songs, the way my parents looked at me — all of it reminded me of who I was beyond the cult.

Patience and appreciative communication

Many relatives despair at how long it takes for a cult member to begin questioning their beliefs. But indoctrination is a slow process, and it doesn't simply fall apart overnight.

Accusations or force rarely help — on the contrary, they often reinforce a person's defensive stance. Instead, empathy, open conversations free of preconceived judgments, and expressing genuine concerns in a caring way can make a difference.

Back then, my mother simply said, "We're worried about you." No accusations. No loud protests. Just honest concern. That kind of communication opened a door in my mind — even if, at first, I only cracked it open a sliver.

Emotional burden on both sides

Relatives and cult members carry a shared emotional weight, even if they experience it very differently. The member may feel fear, guilt, shame, or confusion, while the family struggles with helplessness, anger, and grief. Both sides experience sleepless nights. Open discussions can help channel these feelings and make them more understandable to everyone involved. Joint activities such as walks, short sporting outings, or simply a calm conversation over tea can gradually help break down barriers. Sometimes, my father and I connected by playing tennis together. The physical movement helped release tension, and during the breaks, we cautiously talked about our feelings. Moments like these made me feel less alone.

Subchapter in Brief

FAMILY AND CLOSE FRIENDSHIPS PROVIDE A STEADFAST FOUNDA-
TION, EVEN IF THE CULT TRIES TO WEAKEN THEM. PATIENCE, EMPA-
THETIC COMMUNICATION, AND SHARING THE BURDEN TOGETHER
BUILD TRUST. EVERY RESPECTFUL GESTURE OF RECONCILIATION,
EVERY MEMORY OF THE PAST, EVERY SPARKLING MOMENT OF UNDER-
STANDING LAYS A CORNERSTONE FOR LATER DOUBTS AND, ULTI-
MATELY, FOR LEAVING THE CULT.

9.2 PREVENTIVE MEASURES AND SETTING BOUNDARIES:
RECOGNIZING WARNING SIGNS EARLY

Noticing warning signs

A subtle yet steady change observed from the outside can be a hint that a loved one is falling under the spell of a cult. Sudden changes in behavior, rigid beliefs, withdrawal from former interests, constant secretiveness, or un-explained financial strains — all of these are serious indicators. I, too, began to withdraw, gave up my usual hobbies, and talked only about the "new truths." My family noticed that I avoided questions, canceled meetings, and became nervous when certain topics came up.

Using external perspectives and knowledge

Before reacting hastily, it's wise to first get your own picture of the cult's methods and dynamics. Specialist literature, counseling centers, and online information sources offer factual insights that can help you pose gently critical questions instead of applying thoughtless pressure. Today, I know that my sister took this path. She read books by former members and reached out to a counseling center. This prepared her to show understanding rather than confronting me head-on.

Clear boundaries and protective measures

Even though empathy and understanding are important, that doesn't mean you have to accept everything without resistance. If you're offering financial support, you should carefully consider whether it indirectly strengthens the cult. Maintaining neutrality while also upholding clear values and limits is crucial. A statement like, "I support you, but I won't give any financial support to your group," conveys firmness without being judgmental. When my parents made it unmistakably clear that they wouldn't pay for the cult's expensive "seminars," I felt their resolve. They drew a firm line without rejecting me as a person.

Education as prevention

The more relatives know about the mechanisms of cults, the earlier they can intervene. Helpful resources — such as podcasts, videos by former members, factual articles, and professional counseling services — enable people to recognize manipulative structures more easily. This knowledge provides a foundation for acting calmly and avoiding impulsive reactions. It forms a stable basis from which relatives can better reach their loved one.

Subchapter in Brief

RECOGNIZING WARNING SIGNS EARLY, INFORMING YOURSELF, AND
SETTING CLEAR BOUNDARIES — THESE STEPS CREATE A STABLE
FOUNDATION FOR DISRUPTING SLOW-BURN MANIPULATION. EDUCA-
TION AND PRUDENT ACTION PROTECT BOTH SIDES.

9.3 LONG-TERM STRATEGIES: PERSEVERANCE, SELF-CARE, AND NEW OPPORTUNITIES

Maintaining a long-term perspective

Leaving a cult is rarely a spontaneous decision — doubts typically creep in gradually. Relatives should remember that pressure or forced confrontations can actually delay this process. Instead, it's the small gestures and moments of recognition that make a difference. Eventually, my parents realized they couldn't persuade me. Rather than pushing me, they simply made space — continuing to invite me to family gatherings and showing genuine interest in my life outside the cult's teachings. Years later, I recognized just how valuable their patience and persistence had been.

Protecting one's own emotional health

For relatives, this situation can become a severe test of endurance — feelings of guilt, self-blame, and exhaustion are entirely normal. However, to avoid spiraling into emotional burnout, it's essential that they prioritize their own mental well-being — pursuing hobbies, taking breaks, seeking counseling, and openly discussing their feelings.

Those who remain stable within themselves can be a reliable anchor in the long run. Back then, my family turned to a counseling center for support. This step gave them a space to express their fears and encourage each other — without seeing me as "the enemy."

Making use of networks and cultural resources

A strong support network — within and beyond the family — is a valuable asset. Shared celebrations, family traditions, and cultural festivities offer opportunities for the cult member to experience a sense of normality.

Even if the invitations are initially turned down, the gesture alone conveys a sense of belonging.

I remember a New Year's Eve party my family invited me to. The casual, joyful atmosphere, the laughter, the toasts — all of it made me feel that there was life beyond the tension.

Celebrating small steps

Every tiny move toward openness is cause for celebration.

For instance, if a cult member is willing to talk about what's going on in the group or attends a family dinner, that effort should be acknowledged. Positive feedback, gratitude, and sincere interest act like beacons — signaling that outside the cult, a loving space is waiting.

I still remember the first time I truly laughed again in front of my family. They didn't take it for granted. They recognized the moment, appreciated it, and let me feel their joy. And deep inside, I felt it too.

Subchapter in Brief

PATIENCE, SELF-CARE, A RELIABLE NETWORK, AND CELEBRATING
SMALL STEPS CULTIVATE THE GROUND FOR SUSTAINABLE CHANGE.
A CULT MEMBER'S PATH BACK TO SELF-DETERMINATION TAKES TIME,
BUT CONSISTENT PRESENCE, UNDERSTANDING, AND RECOGNITION OF
EVERY SMALL PROGRESS PAVE THE WAY TO A FREE, SELF-GOVERNED
LIFE.

Chapter in Brief

Patience and Understanding

CULT MEMBERS ARE OFTEN THEMSELVES VICTIMS OF INTENSE MANIP-
ULATION. BLAME OR PRESSURE REINFORCES THEIR DEFENSES, WHILE
EMPATHETIC EXCHANGE OPENS DOORS.

Emotional Support

SPEAK OPENLY ABOUT FEELINGS, CREATE SPACES FOR DIALOGUE,
CONSIDER PROFESSIONAL HELP. EVERYONE INVOLVED IS EMOTIONAL-
LY BURDENED AND DESERVES TO BE HEARD.

Recognizing Early Warning Signs

NOTICEABLE BEHAVIORAL SHIFTS, SECRETIVE MEETINGS, OR EXTREME
BELIEFS ARE SERIOUS ALARM SIGNALS. BEING ALERT MEANS YOU
CAN INTERVENE SOONER.

Setting Boundaries and Using Knowledge

CLEARLY COMMUNICATE YOUR OWN VALUES, GET INFORMED, AND
SEEK ADVICE TO AVOID UNINTENTIONALLY SUPPORTING THE CULT.
CLEAR LIMITS SHOW STRENGTH WITHOUT JUDGMENT.

Long-Term Strategies

PATIENCE AND ENDURANCE ARE KEY. CELEBRATE SMALL SUCCESSES,
KEEP A LONG-TERM PERSPECTIVE, AND GIVE BOTH YOURSELF AND
THE CULT MEMBER TIME. MAINTAIN YOUR OWN INNER STABILITY IN
ORDER TO PROVIDE A SOLID FOUNDATION FOR THE RETURN JOUR-
NEY.

WHAT FAMILY MEMBERS CAN DO

This chapter shows that while relatives cannot control everything, their steady attention, understanding, and inner strength can make a significant impact. They offer a safe harbor that eases the journey back to a free, self-determined life. Experience shows that quiet, loving presence often accomplishes more in the end than even the most forceful argument.

Chapter Ten

EPILOGUE

When I look back today, I feel mainly relief and inner peace. Since my exit, the cult is no longer part of my life — no letters, no messages, no demands, no new attempts to track me down. I am free. This freedom feels like an untouched, wide-open space where I can finally be myself again — without manipulation, without pressure, without the subtle threads that groups use to bind their members, even when they don't outwardly appear to be cults.

But this freedom was not a gift. It is the result of personal decisions, internal struggles, and the steadfast support of those closest to me. My wife, Valentina, stood by my side through those difficult years. Together, we endured this crisis and discovered just how deep our bond truly was. Our eventual marriage was no casual promise — it was an expression of our matured strength, our trust, and the love that held us together despite everything. Today, we both know that love is anything but weak — it is a force that heals wounds, brings clarity, and opens new horizons.

For the relatives of cult members, my experience can be difficult to understand — especially when it involves groups with no well-known name, those that operate in secrecy, or those that don't present themselves as established cults. The danger is often recognized only when a child, partner, or best friend is already entangled in its structures. That's when powerlessness sets in — confusion, uncertainty about whether or how you can help. In these moments, it is crucial to recognize that compassion does not mean abandoning all boundaries. On the contrary, genuine love encourages but does not excuse every action. It offers a hand without trying to save someone at any cost. Hope and clarity must go hand in hand — it is possible to show understanding while still maintaining a firm position.

What ultimately helped me was not just the care shown by others but also my own decision to accept reality and take responsibility for my life. It required the willingness to reflect on myself and the courage to step into the unknown. For relatives, this means: You cannot take every step for those affected, but your love can serve as a reliable anchor when they are ready to free themselves from the cult's invisible net. This love does not guarantee a quick exit, but it sends a clear, constant message:

I'M HERE WHEN YOU NEED ME. I BELIEVE IN YOU, EVEN IF YOU CAN'T BELIEVE IN YOURSELF YET.

I see this epilogue not only as the conclusion of my story but also as a message to the relatives and friends of cult members: Never give up hope, but don't cling to illusions. Understand that cults can creep into your loved ones' lives without you even realizing it. Talk openly about your concerns, gather information, and seek help from counseling centers or support groups. Remember that your compassion can be unconditional without tolerating abuse.

In the end, love is the key. It is quiet, not intrusive; patient, yet allowing room for change. It provides support without binding and courage without coercion. With that love in your heart, you can keep a certain distance when necessary — without abandoning the person.

When the time comes for your loved one to break free from those shackles, this love will shine like a lighthouse in the night — a beacon in the darkness, guiding them back to life.

EPILOGUE

Kapitel Elf

GRATITUDE

At this point, I would like to pause and thank everyone who accompanied and supported me on my journey — whether through a listening ear, tangible help, or simply their presence during difficult times.

First, my deep gratitude goes to my wife, Valentina. You were not only a witness to one of the most challenging phases of my life but also an unwavering pillar of strength and confidence. Your patience, your empathy, and your constant readiness to accept me as I am showed me that love, even on shaky ground, can still provide the strongest support. Without you, this path would have been immeasurably harder.

I thank my family for the home you have always offered me — a place where I was received with open arms, no matter how tangled my life became. Your forgiveness, warmth, and unconditional support showed me that family bonds can be stronger than doubts, crises, or alienation. You demonstrated that a shared history, memories, and a sincere "We're here for you" can heal deep wounds.

I also extend my gratitude to my friends and acquaintances — both old friends, who helped me cross old bridges into the past once more, and new friends, who taught me that it's worth opening up to others again. Your willingness to listen, your questions, your thoughtful silence, and your relentless sense of humor helped me feel part of a vibrant community. You gave me back a sense of normality that I sorely missed in those years.

A special thank you goes to those whose names might not appear in this book: counselors, therapists, lawyers, and representatives of aid organizations, exit networks, and support groups. Your expertise, humanity, and practical assistance not only helped me navigate a safer path out of the cult but also helped me understand what had happened to me. Without your clear voices and knowledgeable advice, I could easily have lost my way in the darkest stretches of my journey.

Lastly, I would like to thank the readers who are willing to engage with my story. Your openness, willingness to grapple with this challenging topic, and desire to better understand it are invaluable. If even one person gains hope, learns to set better boundaries, or finds new courage from reading this, then this book has fulfilled its purpose.

To everyone who, in some way, contributed to my liberation and healing — directly or indirectly, visibly or invisibly, loudly or quietly — I offer my sincere gratitude. Your empathy, patience, love, and humanity form the foundation on which my present freedom, stability, and joy in life rest. For that, I am deeply thankful.

Chapter Twelve

APPENDIX

12.1 CHECKLIST FOR RELATIVES TO RECOGNIZE POSSIBLE SIGNS OF CULT INVOLVEMENT

This checklist offers guidelines that can help you detect potential signs of cult membership early on and respond sensitively.

1. CHANGES IN BEHAVIOR AND PERSONALITY

- Does your relative withdraw emotionally? Do they seem more distant or closed off than before?
- Are they showing noticeable mood swings, excessive anxiety, or nervousness?
- Have they suddenly lost interest in hobbies, friendships, or career goals?

2. CHANGES IN SOCIAL ENVIRONMENT

- Has your relative significantly reduced contact with longtime friends and family?
- Have they mentioned new "friends" or a new group that has become especially important to them?
- Do they suddenly refer to family or old friends as negative or "harmful"?

3. COMMUNICATION

- Do they evade questions about their new social connections or beliefs?
- Has their way of speaking changed? Are they increasingly using new terms unfamiliar to you or repeating phrases from the group?
- Do they refuse to share information about their activities, or become irritated when you ask?

4. TIME AND FINANCIAL COMMITMENTS

- Are they spending an unusually large amount of time on new activities, meetings, or seminars?
- Are they investing financially in the new group or selling personal property?
- Are there significant financial demands or pressure to invest more time in the group?

5. IDEOLOGICAL SHIFTS

- Do they suddenly have new beliefs or spiritual views radically different from their previous ones?
- Are they engaging in strong black-and-white thinking (e.g., the outside world is bad, the group is the only solution)?
- Do they feel "chosen" or refer to exclusive knowledge available only within the group?

6. DEPENDENCE AND CONTROL

- Are they increasingly basing their decisions on the group's opinions or instructions?
- Are major life decisions (job changes, moves, relationship matters) heavily influenced by the group?
- Have they spoken about strict rules they need to follow, and do they feel afraid of possible consequences if they break them?

7. RED FLAGS WITHIN THE GROUP ITSELF

- Is there a charismatic leader who is excessively revered?
- Are dissenting views suppressed, or are critical questions seen as threats?
- Is there strong distrust of outsiders or established institutions?

8. PERSONAL PERCEPTION

- As a relative, do you feel excluded, unsettled, or emotionally manipulated?
- Do you sense that your loved one is trapped in fear or guilt?

WHAT YOU CAN DO:

- Remain patient: Don't respond with accusations; listen empathetically.
- Ask gentle questions: Show interest in their experiences without directly attacking the group.
- Offer supportive options: Provide a safe space where your relative can speak freely, without pressure.
- Seek professional help: Contact experts on cult exits if the situation escalates.

12.2 STEP-BY-STEP PLAN:
SAFELY LEAVING A CULT AND MAKING A FRESH START

This checklist provides a structured guide for planning and carrying out a successful exit from a cult. It addresses practical considerations (such as security measures, housing changes, and financial independence) as well as the emotional and social challenges that come with such a move.

1. PREPARING TO LEAVE

- Gather information: Understand the cult's dynamics and tactics to assess your situation.
- Build contact with trustworthy individuals: Confide in friends or family members outside the cult's sphere of influence.
- Seek legal counsel: Get advice on any legal aspects, e.g., property claims, financial demands, or protective measures.
- Plan the logistics of your departure, including safe housing and alternate communication methods.

2. ENSURING SAFETY

- Change phone number: Get a new number and share it only with trusted contacts.
- Change your address: Officially register a move and protect your new address (for example, by requesting an address block).
- Protect personal data: Change passwords for email, social media, and bank accounts; use two-factor authentication.
- Designate a safety contact: Choose someone who will regularly check on your well-being.

3. ORGANIZATIONAL STEPS

- Secure a safe place to stay: Find housing away from the cult's reach, such as with friends, family, or in a shelter.
- Achieve financial independence: Open your own bank account and set aside funds for basic needs.
- Gather important documents: Collect your passport, ID cards, birth certificate, insurance paperwork, and other essential papers.
- Sever ties with cult resources: Cancel subscriptions, memberships, or obligations linked to the cult.

4. EMOTIONAL AND PSYCHOLOGICAL STABILIZATION

- Seek professional help: Arrange appointments with a therapist experienced in cult exits.
- Join support groups: Connect with others who plan to leave or have already left a cult.
- Practice self-care: Incorporate activities that bring you joy, such as exercise, meditation, or hobbies.
- Reflect on past experiences: Start keeping a journal to process thoughts and feelings.

5. OVERCOMING ISOLATION AND FINDING SOCIAL SUPPORT

- Build new networks: Seek out clubs, courses, or volunteer work unrelated to the cult.
- Strengthen existing relationships: Explain your situation to your family or friends, if possible, and ask for support.
- Limit contact with cult members: Break it off or reduce it to the bare minimum.
- Have open conversations: Share your new boundaries and ask for understanding if relapses occur.

6. LEGAL STEPS AND LONG-TERM SECURITY

- Implement protective measures: Look into legal options such as restraining orders or no-contact orders.
- Get legal help with demands: Consult a lawyer on any financial, legal, or contractual claims the cult might make.
- Secure testimony: If the cult has acted illegally, consider gathering evidence and filing a report.
- Consider new identity options: In extreme cases, state assistance may help you maintain secure anonymity.

7. PLANNING A NEW BEGINNING

- Set clear goals: Reflect on your personal and professional objectives.
- Develop your skills: Enroll in courses or training programs to learn new abilities.
- Strengthen independence: Work toward reducing reliance on external influences, both emotionally and financially.
- Seek ongoing support: Stay connected with aid organizations or groups that foster a sense of stability.

12.3 CHECKLIST: RETURNING TO A SELF-DETERMINED LIFE

Below is a checklist that can help former cult members reclaim a self-determined life. It covers practical steps to support emotional, social, and professional reintegration:

1. EMOTIONAL PROCESSING

- Seek psychological help: Schedule an appointment with a therapist or counselor specializing in cult exits.
- Encourage self-reflection: Keep a journal to process thoughts and emotions.
- Address trauma: Look into therapeutic approaches like EMDR if you've experienced traumatic events.
- Be patient with yourself: Understand that healing is a process, and setbacks are normal.

2. REBUILDING SELF-CONFIDENCE

- Identify your strengths: Make a list of your abilities and achievements, even small ones.
- Set small goals: Start with realistic tasks — for example, regular walks or learning a new skill.
- Develop positive routines: Integrate daily rituals like morning meditation or journaling.

3. SOCIAL CONTACTS AND SUPPORT

- Reconnect with old relationships: Reach out to trusted friends and family.
- Create new networks: Attend local community events, courses, or hobby groups.
- Find support groups: Join self-help communities or networks for former cult members.
- Set healthy boundaries: Practice saying "no" and maintain only relationships that uplift you.

4. NEW ORIENTATION IN DAILY LIFE

- Secure financial stability: Review your finances and draft a plan for self-sufficiency.
- Establish a routine: Structure your day with set times for work, leisure, and rest.
- Build independence: Take responsibility for daily decisions, from grocery shopping to larger projects.

5. PROFESSIONAL REORIENTATION

- Revisit your interests: Consider what genuinely interests you and brings fulfillment.
- Use opportunities for continuing education: Sign up for courses or training to develop new skills.
- Seek career counseling: Consult professionals to find the right career path.

6. LONG-TERM PERSPECTIVES

- Define long-term goals: Imagine where you want to be in five or ten years.
- Celebrate victories: Recognize your progress, no matter how small.
- Accept setbacks: Understand that occasional relapses may happen — what matters is getting back on track.

7. SELF-PROTECTION

- Keep your distance from former cult members: Avoid contact with toxic individuals or groups.
- Remain alert to manipulation: Learn how to identify and avoid manipulative behavior.
- Develop an emergency plan: Prepare a safety net for difficult situations, including supportive contacts.

"Love conquers all;

let us, too,

yield to love"

VERGIL

AUTHOR BIOGRAPHY

Tom Herzberg, a pen name, represents an author who spent eight years in a cult before taking the brave step toward freedom. With his personal insights into manipulative structures and practical support strategies, he now helps both those affected and their loved ones find a path to liberation and renewed hope.